Praise for The Pursuit of Abso

This book and the accompanying workbook are must 'read-and-engage' tools for top financial advisors and their teams, and also for those aspiring to become top advisors. Julie knows this space first hand as an entrepreneur herself, and applies much of what she's learned about what's most important, both personally and professionally, to drive Absolute Engagement. She's presented the information in a way that enables the reader to go to work, with Absolute Engagement in their firm and their life as an expected outcome. Once you get started with the exercises at the end of chapter one, you won't want to put it down.

-David Patchen
SVP, Education and Practice Management, Raymond James

This is a brilliant 21st century business book that will help financial services entrepreneurs get back to what they love. As I read it I was constantly reminded and re-focused on the things that really matter; client engagement, the higher purpose underpinning any business, and the importance of keeping balance and good health as part of the journey. It's been written by a person who knows her subject inside out and has clearly lived it too. I'd recommend it to all advisers.

-Brett Davidson
Founder, FP Advance Ltd

Too often we are just doing the work and we don't actually engage with our business to figure out what's meaningful and relevant. Julie Littlechild has managed to capture all of the most important considerations and boil them down to an understandable step-by-step approach to making change. Filled with education, information, insights and action-oriented assessments to complete, this book inevitably leads you to important "ah-hahs!" that allow you to create a vision and execute on it. Well written and thoughtful, it's an easy read but – if you follow Julie's steps – it will most definitely have significant impact on your practice or firm.

-Beverly D. Flaxington, The Human Behavior Coach*
Co-Founder, The Collaborative

I wish Julie had written this book several years ago. As long-time, single-company business owner, I have at times struggled with many of the concepts Julie addresses in this book: the push/pull between business and personal commitments, periods of quiet discontent or downright frustration, breakthrough and the triumph of success – and still, at times, wondering if when I look back at my life I'll be 100% happy with the choices I've made, the chances I took, and the impact I made over the course of time. Written in a conversational, engaging way, this book confirms what I've known for many years: Julie Littlechild is a wise and measured person with terrific insights to share. If you want to push past "the fulfillment flat line", read this book and consider her advice."

-Marie Swift
President and CEO, Impact Communications, Inc.

A fabulous collection of insights, ideas and tips in order to truly achieve the life and the business that you want. With a combination of facts, guidance and personal exercises, the book absolute engages and certainly hits the spot.

-Michelle Hoskin (Little Miss WOWW!™)
Standards International

Being in your own business is a very personal experience. It starts with a dream and if you're lucky the dream evolves into an extension of you, your value systems and beliefs. Through this journey you get a chance to impact the lives of customers, employees, suppliers and most importantly yourself.

Too often business owners let their vision be co-opted into something they don't recognize. Following Julie's formula for first starting with personal vision and then actively designing your service delivery system will help you get the right clients and customers every time. This is the formula that I've used for myself over the past 40 years and it's the one that lets me come to work every day with excitement and passion about what I do and who I serve.

Read this book, do the exercises and find your own path that will add value to you and your customers. You'll be glad you did.

-Josh Patrick
Founding Principal, Stage 2 Planning Partners

I have been coaching financial advisors for 25 years. During that time, I have often referred them to Julie Littlechild's research on Client Engagement. For much of that same 25 years, I have been hoping that Julie would share her insights in a book, so they would become more widely known. The truth is, however, that I am glad she waited until now, because the value of her knowledge has just increased exponentially.

Within The Pursuit of Absolute Engagement, Julie elevates the concept of "engagement" to a whole new level of meaning as a powerful force in the development of an advisor's vision for their life as well as their business. It is the perfect foundation on which to build a truly "engaged" practice. I now have a potent, yet very practical addition to my coaching tools. Thanks Julie!

-George Hartman
President & CEO, Market Logics

With The Pursuit of Absolute Engagement, Julie Littlechild gives advisors the key to a better business and a better life—and has figured out how you can make the two go together. What a wake-up call! Every advisor should read this book!

-Marion Asnes
President, Idea Refinery LLC

The secret to a more successful business is client engagement. And the secret to client engagement is for you to be fully engaged in your business. In The Pursuit of Absolute Engagement, Littlechild takes you step by step through creating a vision and putting together the right clients, the right service mix and the right role so you can be fully engaged in your vision. Overcome the pressures of overwork, difficult clients, management and competition. When you have a business and a role that inspires you, you will be inspiring.

- Steve Wershing
President, The Client Driven Practice

THE PURSUIT OF ABSOLUTE ENGAGEMENT

INTENTIONALLY DESIGN A BUSINESS THAT SUPPORTS THE LIFE YOU (REALLY) WANT TO LIVE.

JULIE LITTLECHILD

Library and Archives Canada Cataloguing in Publication

Littlechild, Julie, author

The pursuit of absolute engagement : intentionally design a business that supports the life you (really) want to live / Julie Littlechild.

Includes bibliographical references.

ISBN 978-0-9958058-0-4 (softcover)

1. Investment advisors--Marketing.
2. Financial planners--Marketing.
3. Financial services industry--Management.
4. New business enterprises--Management.
I. Title.

HG179.5.L58 2017   332.6'2   C2016-907627-X

Printed and bound in Canada

For Liam

I began writing this book, in my head, the day you were born. It was the day I fully understood what was most important. It was also the day I began to lay the foundation for the life that I wanted and needed so that I could be the example that you would want and need.

I hope that you find what you love to do and give yourself permission to follow that dream. As you do, remember to aim high, be brave and keep trying. And in the process, don't forget to be kind to yourself and love as deeply as you are loved.

CONTENTS

INTRODUCTION

The 20-mile marker was nondescript. You might have walked by it without noticing, but for me it may as well have been lit up with fluorescent lights and a disco ball. I was about to take a step beyond the furthest I had *ever* walked.

I was so far behind my team I wondered if they'd already finished and taken a nap. But every now and then I caught a glimpse of one of them in the distance. I saw the words on the t-shirts we'd made for the day that said **'If Not Now'** in bright bold letters. And I took another step and another, and slowly and in great pain, I crossed the finish line. I had walked a marathon. It was one of the first steps (or first 70,000 steps to be exact) that marked a significant change in my life.

It was that day that I fully understood that extraordinary change is possible. While that walk might have felt like a walk in the park for some, it was my Mount Everest. I didn't believe I could do it because somehow I had come to believe that my future had some sort of linear relationship to my past. But the day I decided that I wanted a different future and began to train, I changed that trajectory completely.

Since that time, I've been painfully aware of how easy it is to stay on the same path, whether that's in business *or* life. This is particularly true if you've achieved some level of professional success. Things aren't bad, right? And if things aren't bad, your primary goal is to maintain that level of success, which means focusing on incremental growth. If things aren't bad, you probably don't stop and ask yourself if there's something more. You probably don't ask yourself what you *really* want to create.

But some *have* stopped and asked those questions. They're *Absolutely Engaged* and they've made the decision to intentionally build businesses that support the lives they really want to live. More than that, they're equally intentional about creating lives that fuel their capacity to do just that. Compared to the average professional, they're more financially successful, more confident in their futures, more productive, less stressed, more energized and even more healthy. I've studied them, I've talked to them and I've uncovered what's different in their approach to business and life. In this book, I'll share their stories and give you a blueprint for a business that's both wildly successful *and* deeply fulfilling.

The research is important, but I've also *lived* the pursuit of Absolute Engagement. One day, two years ago, I sat in my office and found myself asking an unfamiliar question. What did I really want to do? I'd achieved some level of success, so the question seemed almost out of place. I thought about other moments that had set me on a new path. There was the day I decided to sell my first business – moments after my son was born and driven by a desire to have more time with him. There was that 20-mile marker and the courage it took to take another step and achieve something new and different, casting myself in a new light. I felt like that day in my office was another one of those forks in the road that, if not taken, would mean I'd end up with a business that appeared successful but didn't reflect what I most wanted to do. I'd never given myself permission to ask what I really wanted, because I couldn't envision how I could step off the treadmill that I'd created. I'd convinced myself that *I* was responsible for everyone and everything around me and didn't have the luxury of change. I didn't realize it at the time, but that day Absolute Engagement.com was born.

This book is the culmination of the research, thinking and talking I've done over the last two years. On the following pages, I'll ask you to think about a future that's significant and provide you with a roadmap to take action. We'll work through a step-by-step process and stop to think, long and hard, about your business along the way.

I *want* to make you uncomfortable, but in a good way. I hope the book causes you to question what you want your business (and your life) to look like and to realize that you need to intentionally create that future. I hope you take the first step toward Absolute Engagement. (It's worth it.)

Julie

THE STARTING BLOCK

On a race track, the starting block is designed to give sprinters the benefit of a powerful burst forward from a four-point stance. A good start puts the runner in a stronger position relative to everyone else and helps them reach their top speed faster. I hope this book is your starting block, a tool you can use to achieve both meaning and momentum.

On the following pages, I'll map out a plan to help you achieve Absolute Engagement, drawing on research from some extraordinarily successful advisors. Along the way, I'll ask you to think about your business, your life and your future. You'll find new research, stories from your peers and, most important, exercises to help you take action.

Defining what you want to create demands introspection and that's not something we can typically schedule between meetings, while eating a sandwich at our desks. It almost demands that you take yourself out of your day-to-day environment and create space to think. If you can commit to working through the questions in this book and give yourself the space to really think about what you want to create, that will be the biggest step forward to an utterly fulfilling future.

A Quick Road Map:

Chapter 1: You'll examine where you are today and the pressures that can build to make your business and life good but not great.

Chapter 2: I'll introduce the concept of Absolute Engagement as a new standard that will help you build a business that is growing and incredibly fulfilling. And you'll look at the impact of doing just that.

Chapter 3: You'll examine the principles that inform the businesses of those who have achieved Absolute Engagement. More important, you'll review the five steps to getting there and the critical decisions you'll need to make along the way.

Chapter 4: You'll get real about what is most important to you and craft a personal vision that will become the core of the future of your business.

Chapter 5: You'll translate that personal vision into a business vision that will drive how you work with your clients and your team.

Chapters 6 – 9: In these important chapters you'll walk through how to take action, and map out a client and team experience that is completely aligned with your personal vision.

Chapters 10–11: You'll focus on how you can ensure that you have the personal capacity and energy to design the business you truly want to create.

Chapter 12: You'll review your commitments and ensure that you have a plan in place to take action.

You'll also find helpful summaries of all the key chapter points as well as exercises in chapters 13 and 14.

As you get to the end of each chapter, I'd suggest taking a day or two to respond to the questions, review your answers and come back as needed. Alternatively you may want to read the entire book to see how the steps connect and then come back and complete those exercises later. The way in which you respond to the questions that are included at the end of each chapter will lay the foundation for each subsequent chapter. You can respond to the questions right in the book or use the workbook, which you can download at www.absoluteengagement.com/book, using the code IfNotNow.

Big change demands real commitment and commitment comes from within. It comes from having a clear understanding of your "why"—your why for yourself, for your business and for your clients. The more you can define and connect with the impact of focusing your business around your personal vision, the more likely you'll be to have the energy to stay the course. To that end, think about the impact of having a business that is not only growing, but equally fulfilling.

Onwards!

PART ONE:
A VISION OF
SOMETHING MORE

At some point, even the most successful people come face-to-face with the fact that there may be something more—some fleeting glimpse of a business that is both profoundly fulfilling and wildly successful. So begins the pursuit of Absolute Engagement.

WARNING:
ONCE YOU START,
YOU CAN'T LOOK BACK.

1
LIFE, DISCONTENT AND POSSIBILITY

If you've ever listened to a child talking about his or her dreams for the future, you'll know that kids have an extraordinary ability to describe the unlikeliest dreams as if they were concrete plans. In less than a week my son can shift his focus from architect to circus performer. And despite a somewhat schizophrenic approach to career planning, I love that his conviction doesn't waver. His goal, in that moment, is absolute.

I'm sure the day will come when he realizes that the market for circus performers is limited, at best. At that point, he'll probably set his sights on something a little more mundane. And in that moment, I fear, his complete belief that anything is possible may start to erode. Like the rest of us, he may lose that part of his imagination that can see the dream without the need to self-edit. But this book is about changing all of that.

As adults we build up a remarkable capacity to talk ourselves out of dreams before ever giving them a chance to breathe. You likely started out in this industry with a very clear vision of your future. You'd grow the business and be wildly successful and, of course, equally fulfilled. And the path to achieving that goal seemed to stretch out clearly and straight ahead.

And you got to work….

You had a plan to grow and things went well. You continued to add new clients until you found that the bigger challenge was managing the growth.

At that point you may have hired an assistant and started to build a real team and a real infrastructure. And that's just work. On the home front, you might have married and had a kid or two. Then, my guess is, you found yourself running faster than ever just to keep up.

And here you are, responsible for a team and your clients and your family, and you need to keep that pace of growth precisely because you're responsible for a team and your clients and your family. You're pushing yourself hard (and doing the same to those around you). Some days it feels like you're doing anything you can just to keep your head above water. And just like that, the business is running you instead of the other way around. When did *that* happen?

It's not all bad news. If you can relate to any of this, my guess is that you still love the industry, you're making a great living and helping people in the process. Yet despite all that is good with this crazy, wonderful industry, it can cause you to feel like you're trading off between growth and personal fulfillment.

Choosing Between Growth and Fulfillment

Over the years I've observed a pattern when it comes to growth. Advisors are strong out of the gate, then plateau; they push forward and plateau again. And so the pattern continues, with minor dips and plateaus but generally moving in the right direction. If growth is your only goal, this is good news.

But what if growth isn't your only goal?

Achieving a reasonable level of growth is a bit like working through the first two levels of the hierarchy of needs[1], developed by American psychologist Abraham Maslow. His research suggests that people need to meet lower-level needs, like safety, food and shelter before they can begin to think about higher-order needs like love, esteem and self-actualization. In the same way, sustainable growth creates a foundation for the business and you need to achieve it before you can fully focus on higher-order outcomes, like deep personal fulfillment.

The Fulfillment Flatline

For the first few years of your career, growth and fulfillment probably seemed to move in tandem because you were building something new and achieving the goals you had set. However, I've observed that even while a business is growing at a reasonable rate, fulfillment seems to level off. It's what I call a "fulfillment flatline".

The symptoms of the flatline are evident if not always obvious.

- You probably work harder than most of the people you know, but the work that used to energize you has started to wear you out.

- You love your business, but your days are full of tasks that take you away from the type of work you love to do.

- You aren't exactly jumping out of bed in the mornings to get to work. The snooze button has become your best friend.

- You feel like you're twisting yourself into knots to meet the demands of your family, your clients and your team, and because of that you don't feel like you're doing your best for anyone.

- And, you stopped asking how your needs fit into your day a long time ago.

So here we sit. Life is good, but perhaps not great. You've drifted.

The Causes of Drift

There are three reasons we drift from our intended vision. The most common cause of drift is that life pulls us off course from our original vision, however a lack of vision or a change of heart may also play a role. All three causes are insidious but once identified can be the catalyst for something extraordinary.

1. The One-Degree Effect

Some of us start with clear goals but drift off course—imperceptibly at first. This is what I call the One-Degree Effect. The One-Degree Effect is the cumulative gap between where you are today and where you thought you would be when you started out. It's not, necessarily, the result of significant (or even conscious) decisions. Rather, it's the impact of veering, very slightly, off course over a long period of time.

The easiest way to understand the impact of the One-Degree Effect is to think about a plane's flight path. If you flew from San Francisco to New York and your plane was just one degree off course, you'd go one mile off course for every sixty miles flown. When you disembarked you'd be about 43 miles away from your intended location. That might not sound like a big deal but it would be if you were heading to Manhattan and ended up in Princeton, New Jersey. And that's just one (barely perceptible) degree— 1/360th of a circle. We're often off course by far more than that in our businesses and lives.

When you experience the One-Degree Effect your goals are still there— and they're still tangible and meaningful—but you wonder how you ended up so far off course.

2. Lack of Vision

It's not uncommon to start your career with a clear goal, which you probably expressed in terms of growth, assets or revenue. Having that kind of goal, however is very different from having a vision of the business and life that you want to live. If growth is the only goal, you can take any one of a multitude of paths to get there. And as long as the topline is growing, you're on track. The challenge for many, however, is that path doesn't always lead to the life they wanted to live.

A goal is the outcome you want to achieve (growth, for example). A vision, however, is how you want to achieve it (by doing specific types of work for specific types of clients). The differences between goals and vision are striking.

- You can reach a goal and remain wildly unfulfilled. When you realize a vision, it reflects what's most important in your life.

- You can reach a goal and feel exhausted (or bored) by the process. When you realize a vision you're energized and inspired.

- You can reach a goal by applying any number of tactics and strategies (think throwing strategies against a wall and seeing what sticks). When you realize a vision, it's the result of intentional action and a clear path in a specific direction.

Goal   Vision

There's no doubt that you can grow a successful business without a vision, particularly if size is the primary metric you use to measure success. Vision is, in fact, optional. However, if you want to build a business that's both growing and fulfilling, vision is not an option.

3. Change of Heart

Sometimes the reason for drift is much simpler. You start with a clear vision, but over time you change. Your vision changes, what's important to you changes, how you want to spend your time changes and how you define what you want to leave behind changes. And if you change where you're aiming, you need a new path to reflect what really matters in your life.

The Fork in the Road

The three causes of drift show that fulfillment can take a beating for a variety of reasons. But not everyone flatlines—some break through. Those who break through create businesses that are not only growing, but are equally fulfilling. My hypothesis, which draws on observation, research and a healthy dose of personal experience, is that advisors don't break through because they are lucky, work harder or execute better. They break through as a result of an intentional pause and period of reflection, after which they ask a new question about the future. That period of reflection can be a critical turning point if you just give yourself the time and permission to stop.

When you pause and reflect, the question you ask of yourself changes.

In the past you asked: *"How can I grow the business five, 10 or even 20 percent this year?"*

Now you ask: *"What do I really want to create?"*

The new question—*What do I want to create?*—marks a shift from a pursuit of growth to a pursuit of Absolute Engagement. When you ask that question you're asking yourself what you want the next phase of your life to look like. Do you want more of the same? Or, do you want to work toward a future that's deeply engaging for you, for your clients and for your team, a future that's not just engaging but absolutely engaging?

Crystallization of Discontent

When you arrive at that fork in the road and ask yourself what you want to create, it may feel like an epiphany.

. . . .

Sue van der Linden is a financial advisor in Washington, D.C. She has a successful business, a husband, a young daughter and a passion for horses. Like so many professionals, the couple moved out of the city to a bigger home that they loved. They loved the home but the commute was tough—32 miles each way. Every day Sue woke up early to make the trek, returning at 7p.m. if traffic was cooperative. If not, it was more like 8 o'clock.

One morning Sue describes watching her then seven-year-old daughter sleeping soundly. It was 6:30 a.m. and she was about to wake her up, as she did every morning, so they could get to school and work on time. As she reached down to shake her awake, she asked herself a new question. "What am I doing? I'm waking up a small child just to drive to work."

Not long after, the house was on the market and shortly thereafter the family moved closer to the city, to work and to school. They loved the house they were in and had invested so much of themselves in creating a home. In what seemed like a moment, however, she realized how much she was giving up to have that house and how much the family would gain by having more time that wasn't spent in traffic. It seems like a small change, but it ultimately gave her more time to connect with her daughter and more time to pursue riding, a passion that was put on the back burner while she tried to juggle work, family and a home in a distant suburb.

. . . .

What Sue experienced is an example of what American psychologist Roy F. Baumeister calls the *crystallization of discontent*[2]. Baumeister, a respected academic who has published 30 books and written more than 500 articles, is a professor of psychology at Florida State University.

What felt like an epiphany was, in fact, a moment in which the story became complete for Sue. Leading up to that point there would have been frustrations with traffic, a grumpy child, rushed family meals and an occasional twang of loss because she had given up riding. These disparate issues suddenly came together in a coherent and clear storyline: Living here is making our lives worse, not better. The discontent was crystallized.

Note that in response to that epiphany, Sue didn't suddenly turn her life upside down. It's not as if she gave up her lucrative job as a financial advisor, stayed home and started selling homemade jam to her neighbors. She simply changed one aspect of her world that was getting in the way of greater fulfillment, even if it involved a sacrifice.

Yes, some people pause and realize they should be doing something completely different, but for most of us it's about refining some aspect of our existing business. The epiphany, in my experience, is often quiet—a realization that there's something more and that you need to go down another path. And while that moment might represent the crystallization of discontent, that isn't what triggers action. To take the first step toward change it's not good enough to know what's wrong, you need to be able to visualize a better or different future. Without that skill, discontent remains just that. You need a vision.

A Question of Vision

To understand the impact of vision in our lives, it's helpful to look to the work of renowned psychologist Martin Seligman and others. Seligman is a professor of psychology and the director of the Positive Psychology Center at the University of Pennsylvania. He's widely considered the father of positive psychology, which focuses on exploring human potential or, as some people refer to it, the science of happiness.

One of the theories that Seligman studies is called prospection[3]. Prospection is the ability to envision a better future and it shows up in everything from goal setting to day dreaming. It's that ability to imagine something better that causes us to take action. Seligman's research runs contrary to traditional wisdom, which suggests that human beings are programmed to take action to run from pain. His research suggests that while our decisions are influenced by past experience, we're actually driven to take action based on a positive view of the future.

As you work through the pages of this book and think about the future you want to create, prospection will play a critical role. It's that vision of what's possible and what's positive that will inspire you to put the work in to design the business and life you really want.

What's Next?

When you get to that fork in the road and you pause to ask yourself what you want to create, you have two choices. You can continue on the same path, with the view that more of the same will get you where you want to go. It might be hard work but it's squarely in your comfort zone. Or, you can listen to what you're feeling and make some significant changes.

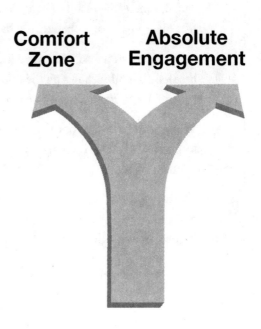

Comfort Zone   **Absolute Engagement**

If growth is your only goal, ask yourself why. If it's simply because you haven't articulated a vision for the future, then let's define that future. The only thing that will change the trajectory you're on is a new vision of what's possible. I'd suggest that the way you get there is by focusing on achieving Absolute Engagement.

The Recap

- As we become adults, we tend to limit our dreams to the clearly achievable. In the process we put limits on our imagination before we give ourselves a chance to dream big.

- We start our careers with a clear goal to grow; managing and sustaining that growth knocks us off course.

- At some point fulfillment flatlines, despite continued growth.

- The flatline is the result of drift from our original goals, lack of a clear vision or a change in what is important to us.

- Some advisors pause, recognize they are off course and break through by changing the question from *"How will I grow?"* to *"What do I want to create?"*

- When you reach the fork in the road, you have a choice to pursue Absolute Engagement or slip back into your comfort zone.

- The pursuit of Absolute Engagement changes the trajectory and focuses you on a future that combines significant growth with profound fulfillment.

Your Turn

This exercise is designed to help you get real on where you are, what you want and what's getting in your way. It's just between you and the book so give yourself the time you need to think, reflect, respond and to come back and change your answers if needed. Let the questions percolate and please recognize that this isn't as easy as you may think, but it's probably much more important than you can imagine.

Download the full workbook at www.absoluteengagement.com/book and enter the code 'IfNotNow'. The workbook includes room to respond and tips to interpret your answers.

To what extent do you agree or disagree with the following statements?

	Not at all. I completely disagree.			Absolutely. I completely agree.	
	1	2	3	4	5
I'm passionate about my business as it is structured today.	○	○	○	○	○
I feel very fulfilled by the actual work I do each day.	○	○	○	○	○
I feel like the work I do has real purpose.	○	○	○	○	○
I feel energized by the work I do.	○	○	○	○	○
I feel in control of how I spend my time.	○	○	○	○	○
I would describe myself as joyful.	○	○	○	○	○

How do you feel about your responses to those questions?

_____

_____

_____

_____

_____

On which statements do you genuinely want to see a higher rating?

_____

_____

_____

_____

_____

Thinking about things you want to change, what caused you to give those statements lower ratings?

_____

_____

_____

_____

_____

Still thinking about the things you want to change, exactly what would need to be different in order to achieve a five out of five? (Hint: you may not know the answer to this and that's ok.)

_____

_____

_____

_____

_____

LIFE, DISCONTENT AND POSSIBILITY

Which of the following describes where you are today, as it relates to your goals and your vision for the business?

○ I'm exactly on track

○ I have drifted from the vision I once had for the business

○ I have clear goals but no clear vision

○ My vision has changed; the things that are important to me have changed

If things have changed, what was your original vision for the business and why do you think you've drifted?

_____

_____

_____

_____

_____

How would you describe the vision you have for your business today?

_____

_____

_____

_____

_____

Thinking about the next phase of your business, what's most important to you?

_____

_____

_____

_____

_____

Which of the following best describes you?

○ I'm always focused on the needs of others

○ I balance the needs of others with my own needs

THE PURSUIT OF ABSOLUTE ENGAGEMENT

If you're always focused on the needs of others, why do you think this is the case and what impact does that have on your life and your business?

_____

_____

_____

_____

_____

How would it feel if you could build a business around your personal vision?

_____

_____

_____

_____

_____

Do you feel you put the right amount of energy into both your business and your personal life?

O Yes

O No

If no, what would it mean if you could be more intentional about your personal life?

_____

_____

_____

_____

_____

Are you open to the possibility that there might be a way to run your business that is more personally fulfilling?

O Yes

O No

LIFE, DISCONTENT AND POSSIBILITY

What scares you the most about making a change to the way you run your business?

_____

_____

_____

_____

_____

I won't ask you to make specific commitments at this point other than to think about what you've written, to focus on what's important and to use that to inform the next step.

2
ABSOLUTE ENGAGEMENT: A VISION OF WHAT'S POSSIBLE

START

STARTING POINT:
You've accepted the possibility of something more, a path that leads toward Absolute Engagement.

To pursue Absolute Engagement is to be intentional about structuring your business in a way that supports meaningful growth. At the same time, it's about ensuring that you have the capacity, energy and passion to stay focused on your goals for the long haul. So Absolute Engagement is about your business, your life and the connection between the two.

The Pursuit of Absolute Engagement

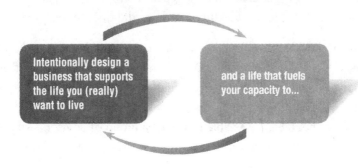

Intentionally design a business that supports the life you (really) want to live

and a life that fuels your capacity to...

I describe Absolute Engagement as an ongoing pursuit—not to wear you out before you even begin but as a recognition that big changes don't happen overnight. Your priorities may shift over time. It's a bit like saying that happiness is an ongoing pursuit—the factors that contribute to happiness may evolve over time but the goal remains the same. You never stop trying to achieve it.

In action, Absolute Engagement is born of an alignment of your personal vision, your business vision and both the client and team experience. When those things are fully aligned, you transform your business from one that's growing to one characterized by both profound meaning and significant momentum.

The Hypothesis

Initially I created the concept of Absolute Engagement as an observer, by watching the approaches of the most successful advisors I met. More specifically, I focused on individuals who had not only built large businesses, but who seemed to have achieved momentum or flow, moving from success to success. They seemed genuinely happier and more fulfilled.

That observation led me to my hypothesis. There is a group of advisors who have structured their businesses in a way that fully aligns the vision they have for their lives with the vision they have for their businesses. The result is that they're laser-focused, grow faster and are more fulfilled. They weren't just engaged, but absolutely engaged. I saw this in action, but I wanted some evidence as to what these advisors did differently.

To understand the drivers of Absolute Engagement I conducted a series of interviews, each of which lasted over two hours. From there I conducted an in-depth, quantitative study among 600 financial advisors who each took the time to describe how they approached both their businesses and their lives. Based on that data, I was able to isolate a group of advisors—about 15 percent of the total—whom I would describe as Absolutely Engaged.

They were Absolutely Engaged because they had designed their businesses in three very specific ways. The impact of the approach they took was staggering, not only on their businesses but their lives.

15 percent of advisors are Absolutely Engaged.

What The Absolutely Engaged Do Differently

Advisors who are Absolutely Engaged have both defined and are living their ideal in three areas.

- **Clients.** They have identified the clients they're passionate about working with, for whom they can do their best work and who need what they want to offer. Just as important, they have successfully built businesses that target these individuals so that the majority (if not all) of their clients fit into this target group.

- **Work.** They have clearly defined the kind of work they want to do for clients—their ideal offer. Just as important, the bulk of the work they do (if not all) reflects this passion.

- **Role.** They have identified the role they want to play on the team, focusing on the activities that they (and they alone) can do to drive the business forward. Just as important, they have structured their businesses and their teams to allow them to focus on that work.

On the next chart you can see how drastically the Absolutely Engaged differ from the other 85 percent of advisors on the basis of these three areas of their business.

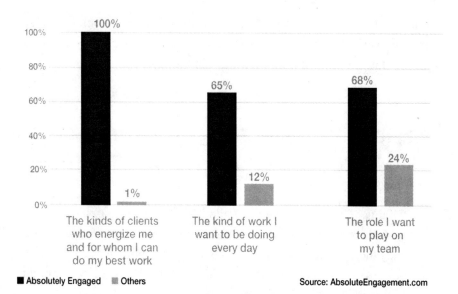

THE PURSUIT OF ABSOLUTE ENGAGEMENT

Source: AbsoluteEngagement.com

Q: Thinking about the following, to what extent have you clearly defined each of the following for yourself? Shows percentage who have both defined and are living the ideal in this area.

Simply stated, the Absolutely Engaged have intentionally designed their businesses around the things they are most passionate about, whether they be: the clients with whom they work, the work they do or the role they play. Combined, these three things represent their personal vision, a reflection of what is important to them.

Those who are Absolutely Engaged use that personal vision to drive the business vision. I don't want to suggest that personal vision is some sort of feel-good strategy. Absolute Engagement starts with personal vision but is just as much about how you execute that vision. Absolute Engagement is like passion with a game plan.

The Impact of Absolute Engagement

We'll explore the path to Absolute Engagement in the chapters that follow. But let's start by reassuring ourselves that the path is worth taking. If you're going to embark on any significant journey, you'll probably want to know what will happen when you get there.

The best way to understand the impact of Absolute Engagement—the impact of doing the three things highlighted earlier in this chapter—is by comparing them to other advisors. The differences are stunning.

Greater Confidence, Clarity and Control

Those who are Absolutely Engaged had greater confidence, clarity and control when it comes to professional goals. They were:

- 1.7x more likely to say they were "very clear" about their long-term professional goals

- 1.6x more likely to say they were confident they would reach those goals

- 1.7x more likely to feel in control of reaching those goals

This higher level of clarity, confidence and control also spills over into the personal goals that the Absolutely Engaged have set.

"This is the proportion of my day that I spend on the things that I should be doing."

53% — Absolutely Engaged

40% — All others

Source: AbsoluteEngagement.com

Greater Focus

When you're clear on your goals, you get clear on how you spend your time. On average, those who are Absolutely Engaged invest more time on the activities that they know will propel their businesses forward.

"I generate $1m or more in annual revenue."

49%

29%

Absolutely Engaged — All others

Source: AbsoluteEngagement.com

Greater Financial Success

When you focus on the activities that drive the business forward, financial success follows. Those who are Absolutely Engaged are 1.7x more likely to be generating $1 million-plus in annual topline revenue in their businesses than those who are not.

"I work fewer than 40 hours a week."

40%

24%

Absolutely Engaged — All others

Source: AbsoluteEngagement.com

More Time Off

With financial success comes the comfort to spend more time away from the office. Those who are Absolutely Engaged are more likely to work fewer than 40 hours a week (and they take more vacation time as well).

Enhanced Sense of Well-being

Focus, financial success and more time off have a net positive impact on your sense of well-being. Those who are Absolutely Engaged are:

- half as likely to feel high stress at work as the others

- twice as likely to report excellent health

- nearly 1.5x more likely to wake up feeling energized

Why Does Absolute Engagement Make Such A Difference?

Absolute Engagement isn't only tied to professional success but to personal well-being and that's exactly what I love about this concept. And, just like you, I wondered why this might be the case.

Part of the explanation for the Absolute Engagement phenomenon might be found, surprisingly, in a small area of Japan called Okinawa. According to Dan Buettner, it's known as a "blue zone," one of the few areas in the world with a very high density of people over the age of 100. Buettner is a National Geographic Fellow who has written several New York Times bestselling books that examine the people who live in these areas of the world and what they do differently. In his TED Talk, *How to Live to Be 100+,* he points out that the average person has the capacity to live to 90 years of age, which means that the average North American is leaving about 12 years of potential life on the table. The Okinawans have reclaimed that lost time, and then some.

While studying the Okinawan people, Buettner learned a lot about food, community and exercise but he also learned some important lessons about purpose. The Okinawan community, it turns out, doesn't have a word for retirement. The concept simply doesn't exist because the goal of work is tied to finding meaning in what you do each and every day. Instead, they have the concept of "Ikigai." Loosely translated, your ikigai is your "reason for getting up in the morning." It's both the source of value in your life and it's something that acts as a lightning rod for action, even if you don't feel inspired in the moment.

When you look at the outcomes associated with Absolute Engagement, it's clear that when you build a business around what is ultimately a personal vision of how you want to live, there's a net positive impact on you and your business. Those who are Absolutely Engaged have created something that represents an elusive combination—a business that is both wildly successful and profoundly fulfilling. My take on this is that it's due, in part, to having focused on something they consider meaningful and valuable—their ikigai.

So now all we need is a path forward and, thankfully, we have one.

The Recap

- Absolute Engagement is about intentionally designing a business that supports the life you (really) want to live and a life that fuels your capacity to do just that.

- About 15 percent of advisors are Absolutely Engaged. They have both defined and are living their ideal as it relates to the clients with whom they want to work, the work they do and the role they play on the team.

- The impact of intentionally designing a business around your ideal work, clients and role includes:

  ° Greater confidence, clarity and control when it comes to professional goals

  ° Greater time spent on the right activities

  ° Greater financial success

  ° The ability to take more time off

  ° Enhanced well-being, including more energy, lower stress and better health

- The reason for such a significant impact is due, at least in part, to creating a business that has clear purpose and reflects what is most important to you.

Your Turn

Advisors who are Absolutely Engaged have experienced a profound effect on their businesses and their lives. They are examples of what's possible, but the path needs to be your own. As a starting point, you may want to assess where you are today as it relates to some of the key components of Absolute Engagement.

Download the full workbook at www.absoluteengagement.com/book and enter the code 'IfNotNow'. The workbook includes room to respond and tips to interpret your answers.

Vision

For which of the following have you defined your ideal AND feel you are living your ideal?

I have defined my ideal client and am working primarily, or entirely, with those clients. ⭕ Yes ⭕ No

I have defined the work I want to do and am primarily, or entirely, focused on doing that work for my clients. ⭕ Yes ⭕ No

I have defined the role I want to play on the team and am spending the majority of my time on the right activities. ⭕ Yes ⭕ No

FYI,
- *100% of the Absolutely Engaged are working with exactly the right clients.*
- *65% of the Absolutely Engaged are doing exactly the right work.*
- *68% of the Absolutely Engaged play exactly the right role.*

Confidence, Clarity and Control

I'm very clear about my long-term professional goals

⭕ Absolutely disagree ⭕ Somewhat disagree ⭕ Neutral ⭕ Somewhat agree ⭕ Absolutely agree

I'm confident that I will reach my long-term professional goals

⭕ Absolutely disagree ⭕ Somewhat disagree ⭕ Neutral ⭕ Somewhat agree ⭕ Absolutely agree

I feel in control of whether I reach my long-term-professional goals

⭕ Absolutely disagree ⭕ Somewhat disagree ⭕ Neutral ⭕ Somewhat agree ⭕ Absolutely agree

FYI,

- *72% of the Absolutely Engaged 'completely agree' they are clear about their goals compared to 43% of all others.*
- *61% of the Absolutely Engaged 'completely agree' they are confident they will reach their goals compared to 38% for all others.*
- *52% of the Absolutely Engaged 'completely agree' they feel in control of reaching their goals, compared to 31% of all others.*

Focus

What proportion of your day do you spend on activities that you, and you alone, should do to move the business forward? _____%

FYI,

the Absolutely Engaged spend 53% of their day on core activities compared to 43% for all others.

Financial Success

What was your total gross revenue in the last 12 months? $_____

FYI,

49% of the Absolutely Engaged generated $1m or more in gross revenue last year compared to 29% of all others.

Time off

How many hours a week do you work, on average? _____hours

FYI,

40% of the Absolutely Engaged worked fewer than 40 hours last week compared to 24% of all others.

Wellbeing

How would you describe your level of stress at work?

○ Very low   ○ Low   ○ Neutral   ○ High   ○ Very High

FYI

37% of the Absolutely Engaged rate their stress level as low or very low compared to 12% of all others.

How would you rate your overall level of health?

○ Poor　　○ Fair　　○ Good　　○ Excellent

FYI,

51% of the Absolutely Engaged report excellent health compared to 25% of all others.

How tired do you feel in the morning?

○ Extremely tired　○ Somewhat tired　○ Neutral　○ Not very tired　○ Not at all tired

FYI,

53% of the Absolutely Engaged report feeling not at all or not very tired compared to 38% of all others.

This assessment is a starting point for the work that you'll do on the path to Absolute Engagement. Like any assessment, it simply helps you see where you are relative to the important outcomes we're seeking. Use this as a benchmark and consider re-assessing your business in 12 months.

3
THE PATH AND
THE PITFALLS

STARTING POINT:
You've set Absolute
Engagement as a goal and
you want to take action.

The path to Absolute Engagement demands self-awareness and self-discipline in equal doses, both things many of us find in short supply. It demands self-awareness because understanding yourself and what you want to achieve is at the core of the process. It demands self-discipline because it requires courage and conviction to make changes to your business, especially when you've already achieved some level of success.

I have looked at the data, drawn on interviews and observed carefully. And, in the process, have identified a defined set of principles, steps and decisions that will move you toward Absolute Engagement. So it's time to focus on action.

The Three Principles

Principles are filters for decision-making. They're at the core of Absolute Engagement because they define the underlying approach to building the business and are consistent for everyone. Exactly which strategies and tactics you apply may differ, based on your unique goals and vision, but the principles remain the same.

Principle 1. Personal vision drives business vision.

Absolute Engagement begins with your personal vision, which comprises the clients with whom you want to work, the work you want to do and the role you want to play on the team. It's that personal vision that informs your business vision, including your ideal client and your offer.

Putting personal vision first might run contrary to how you've built your business to date. Like many advisors you may have started with a business vision and then went straight to work. Despite the fact that you had choices as to how you structured your business, you were probably ill-equipped to understand what a meaningful business was when you started out. You probably found out, along the way, where your passions really lie. Those who are Absolutely Engaged flip the process on its head. They start with a personal vision and then use that to inform the business vision. This doesn't necessarily happen at the outset of their careers but at a point in time when they stop to evaluate the path forward.

For example, your personal vision might be that you love to work with people who are creating value as entrepreneurs. That might translate into a business vision in which you target first-generation business owners.

Principle 2. Your client and team experience should be tailored to actively support your business vision.

If personal vision drives business vision, then everything else needs to fall in line to support that vision. Specifically, your client and team experience should be tailored to align with (and actively support) your business vision, which in turn is a reflection of your personal vision. That means that you can't think about your client or team experience in isolation; both play an active role in bringing your business vision to life. Because you have a clear vision of the clients with whom you want to work and the work you will do, every aspect of the client experience can be tailored to meet the unique needs of that target. Because you have a clear vision of the client experience, you can select and develop a team and culture in a way that aligns with that vision.

For example, with first-generation business owners as your target, you can create a client experience and a team experience that meets their unique needs, including the range of services you provide, the people you hire and the ways in which you communicate.

Principle 3. You're human. Don't forget it.

Sustaining a great business demands accountability and, just as important, it demands renewal. Absolute Engagement is as much about building a business that supports the life you want to live as it is about ensuring that your life feeds your capacity to do the hard work associated with doing just that. This principle reminds us that to take effective action in business we cannot forget the essential ingredients of energy and creativity. And neither can happen without intentional nurturing.

These three principles are at the core of the pursuit of Absolute Engagement because they'll act as filters for decision-making through this process. Now you can begin to peel back the onion, and learn about the actions that will allow you to execute on those principles.

Five Steps and Five Decisions

The three principles provide filters for decision-making but at some point you need to take action. There are five steps that will get you to Absolute Engagement: Awareness, Audacity, Action, Accountability and Renewal. Each step leads to a fundamental decision about how you'll run your business. The way in which you make those decisions will either keep you on the path to Absolute Engagement or send you back to your comfort zone—good but not necessarily great. You'll hear more about each step and specific examples of what it means to take action on each in the following chapters.

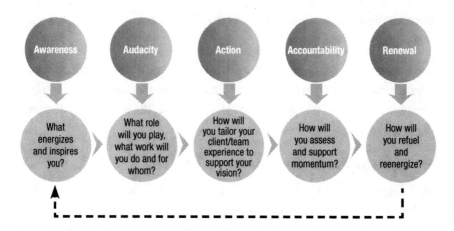

1. Awareness

Awareness is about crafting a personal vision that energizes and inspires you. It's about giving yourself permission to start with a blank slate, one that isn't influenced by how your business looks today or what other constraints you might feel (real or imagined).

This is where possibility lives.

In this step, you'll create a personal vision based on a deeper understanding of what energizes and inspires you.

As you begin to give yourself permission to think about the future you want for your business and your life, you'll be faced with a decision. *Will I use this insight to inform my business going forward or will I push those feelings to the side and slip back into my comfort zone?* Those who are Absolutely Engaged use these insights as the building blocks to design an extraordinary business.

2. Audacity

Audacity is about translating your personal vision into a business vision, a process that may mean breaking with the past and refining your vision for the future.

This is where courage lives.

In this step you'll refine and formalize your target client, your offer and the role you'll play on the team, all in a way that fully reflects your personal vision.

As you begin to define that business vision you'll be faced with another decision. *Will you draw a line in the sand and say to the world that you work with a defined target client to deliver a defined offer? Or will that vision remain a preference as you continue to work with any client who meets your minimum standard?* Those who are Absolutely Engaged clearly communicate the business they are in, on the understanding that it will make them unappealing to some prospective clients and dramatically more appealing to others.

3. Action

Action is about the way in which you engage your clients and your team as well as where you focus your own energies to push the business forward.

This is where confidence lives.

In this step you'll design a client and team experience that is specifically tailored to reflect the needs of your target client, which in turn reflects your personal vision.

As you begin to consider the needs of your target market and the requirements of refining your offer you'll be faced with yet another decision. *Am I willing to change how I communicate with clients and how I recruit and develop my team to ensure that the business reflects the needs of my clients?* Those who are Absolutely Engaged intentionally design the client and team experience to both reflect and actively support their business vision.

The Pivot

As you complete the first three steps you'll find that your business has taken on new life. By aligning personal, client and team engagement you not only drive growth, but also create true momentum. Think of it like a set of gears. When gears move in concert they create power that is greater than the sum of the parts. In the same way, when your business is fully aligned you create a form of torque that propels you forward. The opposite is also true. You'll create friction and a drag on growth if: your client experience is designed to deliver great service but not to meet the needs of a defined target, your hiring practices are focused on technical skills without a focus on shared passion for your target client or if you are working with clients you like but who do not inspire you.

At this point you've structured the business in a way that supports your vision. It's time to turn your attention on yourself.

4. Accountability

Accountability is about ensuring that you have the support you need, personally, to follow through on your goals.

This is where commitment lives.

In this step you'll create a structure to provide you with motivation and support to stay the course on the path to Absolute Engagement.

As you begin to think about how you will find the support you need to stay focused and motivated, you'll be faced with a further decision.

Will I continue to go it alone or will I reach out and create a support network that will ensure I reach my goals? Those who are Absolutely Engaged find formal and informal structures to hold them accountable, help them take action and build an extended team of people who have their backs.

5. Renewal

Renewal acknowledges that in order to sustain momentum you need to refuel and recharge. It's about recognizing (perhaps reluctantly) that we aren't superheroes and need to step back.

This is where creativity lives.

In this step you'll set intentional goals to refresh and renew in order to create the capacity in your life to focus on your bigger professional and personal goals.

As you begin to wonder about your own capacity and energy, you'll be faced with yet another difficult decision. *Will I continue to squeeze in time for myself around the demands of building a business or will I intentionally set goals for renewal in the same way I set goals for the business?* Those who are Absolutely Engaged are as intentional about the time they take off as they are about the time they are working.

The Demons That Conspire to Thwart Your Progress

If the path to Absolute Engagement seems long, it may well be. If the path seems hard, that's also possible. There's no doubt, however, that the path is worth it. As with any journey, there will be potholes along the way and they'll slow you down and cause you to doubt your plan. It's notable, however, that when it comes to Absolute Engagement, those metaphorical potholes are all in our heads. The best we can do is call those demons out so that we have a chance of recognizing them when they appear.

The internal demons are most notable at the beginning and the end of the journey. They stop us from seeing what's possible during the awareness phase and from giving ourselves permission to rest during the renewal phase. Nasty things, those demons.

1. The "Shoulds."

The "shoulds" reflect a natural, but potentially destructive propensity to let our perceived responsibilities dictate our life path.

....

James was an advisor who worked on a very successful team. As much as he enjoyed a lot of what he did, he knew he wanted something different. He wanted to write and to coach and, in the process, to help people by sharing his own experience of battling and surviving depression. He told me that he knew that's what he was meant to do. And while the vision seemed clear, he couldn't imagine making the change because he felt a crushing responsibility to create a comfortable life for his family, which included his four children. His wife had stopped working to raise the children and he felt the weight of family responsibility on his shoulders. Although his wife planned to get back into the workforce, he felt he "should" be the primary financial support for the household, he "should" stick to a job that was predictable and he "should" put aside his own desires to provide for his family.

....

Responsibilities are real but they're rarely as restrictive as we believe. James might have been a better father and husband (and could have made a more meaningful impact on the lives of people around him) if he'd created a plan that allowed him to step off that path and do the work he knew he should be doing. The obligations were real and the children were real so a sudden change would, no doubt, have had a negative impact. For James, things started to change when he realized that everything didn't have to change overnight and he could begin to pursue his dreams while continuing to meet his obligations. He enrolled in a coaching course, began to work on content for his program and started to interview people who fit the bill of those he wanted to help. He talked to his wife about all of this, something he hadn't really done, and the two of them were able to come together on a plan. Importantly, he set a deadline, which was about five years out so that he had a clear path forward and could mitigate the financial risk.

Just like you, I've spent my life and career working very hard. If you asked me why, I would tell you it was for my family. (I have always had a noble cause for killing myself.) Then something happened and it may be a result of age or experience (for me it was when I said good-bye to my forties). I sat back and, with new eyes, examined what I really wanted to do. What was interesting is that the motivations didn't change but I saw a new way to fulfill the same goals. I realized that if I really wanted to do something good for my family, I needed to help myself first. Ironically, by defining and living my biggest possible goals, I not only benefited financially, but became happier and a better role model.

Acknowledge responsibility but don't let it set you on a limiting path.

2. The Armor

Dr. Brené Brown is a professor at the University of Houston's Graduate College of Social Work. She has a unique field of study, focusing on vulnerability, courage, worthiness and shame, and has written three No. 1 *New York Times* best-sellers.

Brown writes eloquently and passionately about the role of vulnerability in our personal success. She defines vulnerability as "uncertainty, risk and emotional exposure." More important, she talks about accepting vulnerability as absolutely necessary to living fully and completely. In one of my all-time favorite Ted Talks, *The Power of Vulnerability* (which has over 25 million views, by the way), Brown documents how we "numb" vulnerability. I believe that this is what we're doing when we put our heads down and keep going instead of asking if there is something more.

Vulnerability, in many ways, is the antidote to a pitfall I see everywhere and which I simply refer to as "the armor." We wrap ourselves in a shield that keeps us tough and focused and marching singularly forward. To accept that you want something different, or to set a big life goal, demands vulnerability because it suggests you may have invested your time and effort heavily in the wrong direction (even if that was a necessary step to getting here). For so many of us it's just easier to stay on the wrong road than to question ourselves. It's the same odd characteristic that stops us from asking for directions when we're lost. Or, perhaps, it's easier not to try because we recognize that failure, even temporary, is a possibility.

The pursuit of Absolute Engagement requires an element of vulnerability because only the vulnerable are willing to ask if they are on the right path. We need to shed the armor.

The Traits That Will Drive Your Success

And just as there are traps to avoid, there are characteristics to nurture. Three of the most important are grit, a growth mindset and big goals.

1. Grit

The concept of grit is gaining significant popularity. According to Caroline Adams Miller, a positive psychology expert, coach, educator and author of *Getting Grit*, grit is an extraordinary quality, despite the overuse of the term. The concept of grit, in an academic setting, was first defined by Angela Duckworth, who in 2013 won a MacArthur Foundation Genius Grant Award for her work. She defined it as "passion and perseverance in pursuit of long-term goals[4]".

One of the things that Duckworth studied, along with Martin Seligman at the University of Pennsylvania, is what separates extraordinarily high achievers from people who are very talented and who, despite that talent, don't seem to be finishing at the top of the pack. They determined that the secret sauce was grit. Among other things, grit predicts who will drop out of West Point and who will win the National Spelling Bee.

The word 'grit' doesn't always belie how important and poignant the concept is in our lives. We're talking here in a business context, but grit is everywhere. It's the single mother who gets up two hours early to study to complete a degree, the father who works three jobs because he wants something better for his family. It's opening yourself up to challenges that seem almost impossible and starting over as many times as it takes because you know the fight is worth the prize. It's what gets you through the toughest times in your life, be that a divorce, a death or what you consider to be an epic failure.

I asked Miller[5] if grit can be learned. She was definitive that yes, it could. "It's true," she says, "that some people are born more optimistic than others. Some people are also born more resilient and some are born more or less impulsive. All of those things play into your ability to keep going, to have a "can do" spirit. But the other half of it is what you choose to think about and do every day.

Miller suggests three strategies to help you up the 'grit' factor in your life and these will be critical in your pursuit of Absolute Engagement:

- **Stress reduction.** Miller says that many of the high achievers she coaches are intentional about integrating things like meditation and exercise into their lives.

- **Your network.** Miller says that gritty people hang out with gritty people. At West Point, she says, their way of dealing with people with low grit scores is to room them with people with higher grit scores. She points out that that is social contagion theory in action and it's brilliant.

- **Optimism.** You can also learn to be more hopeful and optimistic. Many of the uber-successful use coaches to help them nurture this quality. Ultimately grit is about learning the traits of optimism and also hope, and this is a new muscle for many.

At the root of Absolute Engagement is the notion that you need to be conscious and intentional about designing your life. This is a quality that Miller sees as being related to grit. She points to research that shows that the majority of people are very reactive to life. "In order to be a high achiever or a leader, you have to be awake at the wheel of life, which means being proactive. I've never coached anyone to elite performance who didn't become somewhat proactive about how they approached their day." Love it.

In my words, grit is the characteristic that helps us stay focused during the toughest times and bounce back when we're knocked down. It's a concept that was brought to life by a gift my son received one Christmas. It was a blow-up shark with sand at the base. You can whack it with all your might and it bounces back. (Those of us of a certain age will remember this same functionality with Bozo the Clown.) The shark created an interesting demonstration of grit for both my son and the shark. For my son, the grit is apparent as he tries to knock down the shark, seemingly unaware (or not caring about) the physics of the weight at the bottom but committed to winning. And for the shark, well it just keeps popping back up despite the pummeling of a sugar-fueled child.

2. Growth Mindset

As you move along the path toward Absolute Engagement you'll also need to nurture what researcher Carol Dweck refers to as a "growth mindset[6]." Dweck is one of the world's leading authorities on the subject of motivation and is a professor of psychology at Stanford University. A growth mindset refers to the idea that we can grow our brain's capacity to learn and to solve problems. To achieve Absolute Engagement we need to believe that we can learn and change and do things differently.

And what might sound slightly obvious is most certainly not, as Dweck's research uncovers. The key to successful transformation, she found, is about whether you look at ability as something inherent or something that can be developed. Is it a bone or a muscle? In the case of the former, ability is fixed and is something to be "demonstrated." In the latter, ability is "developed" and this is what she refers to as a "growth mindset."

Why is this so important? It's important because in order to take action on a vision that you may have had to pull from the recesses of your brain and heart and dust off, you'll need to develop new skills. You'll start, you'll fail and you'll push forward, but only if you believe that you not only deserve something more, but that you can *learn* how to improve.

Too often we get inextricably stuck in negative beliefs about our own abilities. When I was young my parents bought me a piano and the requisite lessons. It was, in retrospect, one of the best things they could have done for me, although it might not have seemed wise at the time. Let's just say that I wasn't exactly a musical prodigy. I was frustrated and there were tantrums. The tantrums, although I didn't realize it then, were tied to a deep-seated perfectionism that stopped me from learning. The pattern repeated itself in high school. If I couldn't get an A in a subject, I dropped it.

Today, I see grace and wisdom in flailing about and trying to learn something new; in the past I saw imperfection or a feeling of being "less than". Absolute Engagement may push you in a new direction. It will feel uncomfortable at times and you may feel ill-equipped. I promise you this is nothing more than what Michael Hyatt, author, CEO and founder of Michael Hyatt & Co., refers to as the "messy middle[7]." To try is wonderfully awkward and profoundly rewarding.

To pursue Absolute Engagement is to take risks and to believe that you can learn to do things differently. Dweck points to a simple technique she saw used on school report cards. Rather than a failing grade, the report card said "not yet[8]." The children were under no illusions that they hadn't done the work necessary to pass, but the message was clear that they just needed to keep trying rather than accepting the failure as an indictment on their future. When it feels tough, we may need to tell ourselves the same thing.

3. Big Goals

To achieve Absolute Engagement you'll need to set BIG goals. There's a very good chance that incremental change won't get you across the finish line.

- Incremental goals are achieved by tweaking what you're doing today.

- Dreams (quite often) require a fundamentally different approach from how you operate.

There's been a significant amount of research into the concept of setting big goals versus incremental goals, most notably by academics and authors Edwin A. Locke and Gary P. Latham. They had this to say in their book, *New Directions in Goal-Setting Theory*: "So long as a person is committed to the goal, has the requisite ability to attain it, and does not have conflicting goals, there is a positive, linear relationship between goal difficulty and task performance."[9]"

When our goals are modest, we don't apply the same energy. This is due, in no small part, to a distinct lack of inspiration. As a result, we're more likely to settle. Imagine, for example, you set a goal of 15 percent revenue growth in the next year. On the basis of that goal, you tweak your plan from the previous year. You figure out that you can meet the goal if you increase your marketing budget by 10 percent, add a new team member and participate in a course on referrals. At the end of the year, hitting 12 percent growth doesn't look that bad.

The much bigger issue is that only big goals uncover the gaps you need to bridge to reach your goals. Small goals mask those gaps. Let's extend the previous example. You set a goal of growing revenue by 15 percent a year but your long-term goal is to grow the firm to $10 million in annual revenue and you assume the first goal will lead to the second.

The reality is that you can grow by 15 percent a year without making earth-shattering changes to your business model. You need to be focused and do things well, but you can apply a variety of tactics that will give you a good chance of succeeding. However, to run a $10 million business you'll need to think very differently. A goal of 15 percent growth takes you down one path. A goal of becoming a $10 million firm takes you down another.

The bigger goal to reach $10 million would force to you think about whether you have a clear brand, to define your messaging and to evaluate your own skill set in the broader organization. It will force you to invest in the technology and process required to manage a substantially larger client base and team. Those goals would not have emerged if you looked 12 months out at a 15 percent growth goal.

. . . .

Jonathan Hoyle is the CEO of Stanford Brown. When he took on that role, the firm had been achieving respectable growth of 12–15 percent for many years. One day he asked a bigger question of the shareholders. He asked what they really wanted to achieve in the long run. They settled on a very significant growth goal that would see the firm grow to become a $100 million company. With that as a filter, it substantially changed the decisions they made when incremental growth was the goal. They have since moved on to a much bigger and more prestigious office; gotten their own financial services license; staffed up (before needing everyone); made acquisitions; started a graduate recruitment program and hired their own advisors.

. . . .

So we have a big goal, and it's Absolute Engagement. We understand the stunning impact this can have on our businesses and our lives and we have a set of principles and actions to get us there. Now it's time to do the real work. It starts with awareness and creating your personal vision.

The Recap

- Advisors who are Absolutely Engaged approach their businesses with three common principles:

  ° Personal vision drives business vision.

  ° Your client and team experience should be tailored to actively support your business vision.

  ° You're human. Don't forget it.

- There are five steps on the path to Absolute Engagement, each of which brings you up against an important decision:

  ° Awareness is about understanding what really energizes and inspires you when it comes to your clients, your work and your role.

  ° Audacity is about translating your personal vision into a business vision.

  ° Action is about tailoring your client and team experience to specifically reflect your offer and the unique needs of your target, while freeing you up to take on the role that will push the business forward.

  ° Accountability is all about ensuring that you have the support you need, personally, to follow through on your goals.

  ° Renewal acknowledges that in order to sustain momentum you need to refuel and recharge.

- Three obstacles can thwart your progress: focusing on what you think you "should" do, putting on the armor and ignoring the role of vulnerability in defining a vision for the future.

- Three characteristics should be nurtured to help you succeed: grit, a growth mindset and big goals.

Your Turn

The path to Absolute Engagement is defined by three core principals and five steps, each of which leads to a fork in the road and decision to continue or circle back to your comfort zone. As you move through each of the steps, you'll get more granular on what it means, why it matters and how you can take action. For now, take stock of where you are on the path to Absolute Engagement.

Download the full workbook at www.absoluteengagement.com/book and enter the code 'IfNotNow'. The workbook includes room to respond and tips to interpret your answers.

To what extent do you agree or disagree with the following statements?

	Not at all. I completely disagree.			Absolutely. I completely agree.	
	1	**2**	**3**	**4**	**5**
I have a clear personal vision that drives my business vision.	◯	◯	◯	◯	◯
My client and team experiences are tailored to actively support my business vision.	◯	◯	◯	◯	◯
I find ways to support myself, including peer support and intentional relaxation.	◯	◯	◯	◯	◯

THE PATH AND THE PITFALLS

As it relates to the five steps, to what extent would you agree or disagree with the following:

	Not at all. I completely disagree.			Absolutely. I completely agree.	
	1	2	3	4	5
I have a deep understanding of the clients, work and role that energize and inspire me.	◯	◯	◯	◯	◯
I have formalized a definition of my target client, my offer and my role to align with the things that energize and inspire me.	◯	◯	◯	◯	◯
I have designed a client experience that is specifically tailored to reflect the needs of my ideal target client and to engage my clients.	◯	◯	◯	◯	◯
I have designed a team experience that is specifically tailored to support my client experience and to engage my team.	◯	◯	◯	◯	◯
I have the infrastructure and process in place to allow me to focus on the activities that will drive the business forward.	◯	◯	◯	◯	◯
I have a structure in place to provide me with the motivation and support I need to stay the course on the path to Absolute Engagement.	◯	◯	◯	◯	◯
I have set intentional goals to refresh and renew in order to create the capacity I need in my life to allow me to pursue my biggest goals.	◯	◯	◯	◯	◯

THE PURSUIT OF ABSOLUTE ENGAGEMENT

On the basis of your responses, where do you most want to improve?

_____

_____

_____

_____

_____

What impact do you think those improvements will have on your business and your life?

_____

_____

_____

_____

_____

Now let's dig into the 'how to' so you can take action.

PART TWO: PERSONAL VISION DRIVES BUSINESS VISION

Your personal vision defines the work you want to do, for whom, and the role you want to play.

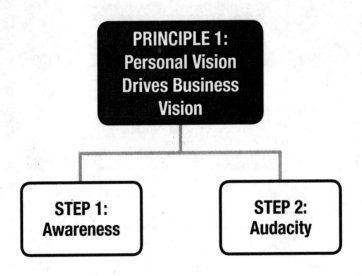

PRINCIPLE 1:
Personal Vision Drives Business Vision

STEP 1:
Awareness

STEP 2:
Audacity

YOUR PATH TO ABSOLUTE ENGAGEMENT

3 PRINCIPLES

1 Personal vision drives business vision.

2 Your client and team experience should be tailored to actively support your business vision.

3 You're human. Don't forget it.

YOUR COMFORT ZONE

ABSOLUTE ENGAGEMENT

STEP 1

AWARENESS
Create a personal vision based on a deeper understanding of what energizes and inspires you.

THE DECISION
Will you use that information to shape or refine your business vision?

IF NO — IF YES

STEP 2

AUDACITY
Translate your personal vision into a business vision by formalizing your target client, your offer and the role you will play on the team.

THE DECISION
Will you draw a line in the sand and say to the world that you deliver a defined offer to a defined target client?

IF NO — IF YES

STEP 3

ACTION
Design client and team experiences that are specifically tailored to reflect your business vision

THE DECISION
Will you change or update how you engage with clients and how you hire, retain and develop to reflect the needs of your target audience?

IF NO — IF YES

STEP 4

ACCOUNTABILITY
Create a structure that will give you the support you need to put your plan in place.

THE DECISION
Will you formalize a process of connecting with peers who will support and push you to succeed?

IF NO — IF YES

STEP 5

RENEWAL
Set intentional goals that support energy and creativity.

THE DECISION
Will you set specific, intentional goals for personal renewal?

IF NO — IIF YES

Complete the steps and you'll be at the intersection of financial success and personal fulfillment. The Absolutely Engaged report higher revenue, less stress, better health and more time spent doing the work they love.

4
AWARENESS: THIS IS WHERE POSSIBILITY LIVES

STARTING POINT:
You have a clear sense of the path to Absolute Engagement and you want to take the first step.

THE NEXT STEP:
Create a personal vision based on a deeper understanding of what energizes and inspires you.

The first principle of Absolute Engagement is that personal vision is the driver of business vision, so it stands to reason that you need to define that personal vision. Awareness is the first step and yes, I'm going to ask you to do a little soul searching here. But stick with me. I'll stop short of asking you about your childhood but I will ask you to think long and hard about what you love or want to do. It's not as easy as it sounds for those of us who've been on a treadmill locked on "just keep going" for most of our professional careers.

Awareness is about getting real about what matters, what you want and how you prioritize those two things. This is where possibility lives! Why? Because you'll be letting your imagination run free, and thinking about your life and work without the perceived constraints of how your business looks today. In this chapter, you'll focus on defining a personal vision that's inspiring and energizing. And while personal vision might seem like a rather nebulous idea, one that can include so many things, our focus is on those three drivers of Absolute Engagement—working with the right clients, doing the right work and playing the right role.

To move through this first step, you'll need to enter the "No-Decision Zone." Being in this zone simply means that I'm asking you to think about what's important to you without trying to figure out if it's possible. It's like a dream without all the analysis. I know that's tough for a group of individuals who are hardwired to be decisive. In fact, if you try to make decisions at this stage you'll probably talk yourself out of the plan before you get started on the path to Absolute Engagement.

The no-decision zone relates back to the example I started with in Chapter 1 and the propensity of my son to dream big dreams. At this stage he's in the no-decision zone. If he tells me he loves to work with animals and wants to be a veterinarian, I don't start talking about the required GPA because it might force a decision too early. If he tells me he wants to be an actor, I don't ask him how he'll overcome his shyness because he might walk away without giving it a chance. This stage is just about the dream for your business and we'll tackle the 'how-to' later.

And here's the spoiler alert: The thinking you do at this stage will ultimately lay the foundation of your business vision.

It's time to Dream, People

Before we talk about what you can do to get started, let's deal with the elephant in the room. The one thing that has the best chance of derailing our efforts is our own thought process. Those of you with young children will be familiar with the Disney Pixar movie *Inside Out*. In that movie, you see a personification of what we experience every day—the complex interplay of our emotions, including anger, sadness, disgust, fear and joy. Just like the little girl in the movie, big kids like us allow those fears and emotions to get in the way of imagining the life we want to live. Those same emotions can get in the way of visualizing a better or different future.

There's no doubt that achieving Absolute Engagement requires a hefty dose of grit and determination. The more I study this concept, however, the more I realize that the challenge of hard work isn't what holds people back. Too often we stumble on the first step—giving ourselves permission to envision a different future and coming to grips with the possibility of something greater for ourselves.

There are so many reasons we stop ourselves from being open to possibility, but three seem to dominate.

- Reaching for a bigger life opens up the possibility of failure. If we don't articulate the dream, we never fail. If we don't seek something more, we're forced to be satisfied with what we have.

- It feels "selfish." Many of us are trapped by a misguided sense of responsibility, one that keeps us moving in the same direction. It's like being on a treadmill without being able to find the off switch. The lucky among us recognize that if we can set goals that inspire us personally it usually makes us a better leader, team member, spouse or parent.

- It requires extraordinary vision. Often, the thing that holds us back is *not* an unwillingness to work hard, but a distinct lack of imagination about what is possible.

Perhaps there's a less dramatic reason that we don't push forward and it's simply that life isn't that bad. Jim Collins is the author and co-author of six books, and my personal favorite is *Good to Great*[10]. In my mind, the first line of that book captures everything that keeps us stuck. "Good," Collins says, "is the enemy of great." What he doesn't explicitly say is that good *isn't that great*. When we settle for what we have simply because we have it—whether that's a business or a relationship—life can feel flat.

This propensity to settle for what we have over what we might have is something that many of us are taught from a young age. My father was a wonderful man and one with many sayings that he'd regularly toss out in conversation. "It could be worse" was a common refrain when I asked him how he was doing. Or, my personal favorite, "I'd complain but no one would listen." In so many subtle ways the message I heard was that you should be thankful for what you have because things could, ultimately, be much worse in your life. Interesting how such an innocuous message can sound positive and yet hold you back. When I talk to my son I want him to feel thankful and grateful for the life he has but never to the exclusion of trying to perfect that life.

So I know you picked up a book about your business and now I'm talking about your feelings and your parents. Don't worry, you're still in the right place if you want to create something meaningful. All of this just highlights the intimate connection between our businesses and our lives. So let's dig in and think about the right clients, the right work and the right role. These combine to create a personal vision that will be at the core of the path to Absolute Engagement.

The Right Clients

In an ideal world your clients would not only need the guidance you can provide but would also be a source of inspiration for you. They'd be the kind of people you are passionate to work with.

Our survey data highlights a direct correlation between working with the right clients and all the positive outcomes associated with Absolute Engagement. All the Absolutely Engaged advisors have defined their target client. More important, they've built their businesses around the unique needs of that target client. Many advisors will say they have a target client but it's the translation of that definition to your messaging, process and infrastructure that's the hallmark of Absolute Engagement.

The reality is that you probably work with many clients who energize and inspire you, some who may drain you and others who are somewhere in between. But what if you worked largely—or perhaps solely—with the kinds of clients for whom you can do your best work? How would it feel to come to work? How would your clients feel about working with you?

As you move through this process I'll be referring to both target clients and ideal clients. They're different; and both play a role in your definition of the clients with whom you want to work. As we go forward when I refer to your target client I'd ask you to think about a client who is both your target and ideal.

- **Target clients.** These are the prospects who are within the potential population of people who are right for your business. For example, you might choose to work with business owners and the total population of business owners will be your target client. However, if you can narrow that definition it will help you focus. You probably aren't passionate about working with just any business owner—perhaps you love to work with entrepreneurs who have started their own businesses.

- **Ideal clients.** These are a subset of your target group. They also possess qualities that are important to you. For example, you may choose to work with entrepreneurs but you only want to work with those who want comprehensive financial planning. Or your ideal might include a match with a client's values. Firms like Ronald Blue & Co., for example, are built to attract clients who share a similar faith.

While I'd suggest that you need to define both your target and ideal, you'll only share the definition of your target client with the outside world. Your target client will become the focus of your marketing and you'll want to communicate that to ensure that everyone knows who you work with. Your definition of an ideal client, however, is more likely to be an internal filter you apply to determine whether a particular prospect is right for your business.

Assume, for example, that you have a passion for working with women in transition. You have defined a target audience and have narrowed it to a segment of the total population of women. Any woman who's going through a life transition, such as a divorce, is technically part of that target audience. If, however, you met with a prospect and she was focused only on investment performance she may not fit with your ideal if you're focused on comprehensive financial planning.

Your ideal client might also include personality traits or characteristics. Not long ago I walked away from a client because I found her personality to be incredibly negative and, for me, this is a deal breaker. The client was in the right industry and I felt I could help but it's incredibly important for me to be in business relationships in which the inspiration goes both ways. That client was part of my target but didn't fit with my ideal.

The challenge with defining your ideal is knowing what is a "nice to have" and what is a "deal breaker." My guess is that you could come up with a list as long as your arm to describe the kinds of people you like working with. The filters that inform your ideal client, however, have to pass a test. If you're willing to walk away from the client if he or she demonstrates that characteristic, then it's part of the definition of your ideal client.

So let's think about who turns your proverbial crank when it comes to clients. The process starts with a question.

Which clients do you most enjoy working with?

When it comes to answering this question, go with your gut. Take out a piece of paper and write down the name of the first 10 clients who come to mind and then ask yourself what these individuals have in common. If you try to respond quickly you might be interested to see who comes to mind without thinking about things like their assets.

Do those clients share:
- The industry in which they work (e.g., mining)
- A profession (e.g., first responders)
- Lifestyle (e.g., boaters)

Do they also share other characteristics:
- Values (e.g., integrity)
- Approaches to investing (e.g., long-term)
- Approaches to advice (e.g., delegators)

Perhaps they're mostly single, married, no children or lots of children. If you look hard enough you'll probably find some important similarities and my guess is that you won't just write down the names of people you like, but of people you've been able to help, who want and need what you offer and who listen to your advice.

You might also tackle this from the other side of the equation and consider which clients drain you of energy. Write down the names of your "anti-ideal" clients and why they came to mind. This will help you set some parameters around the people with whom you don't want to work. Remember, a client can be part of your target market but still not an ideal client for you.

The Right Work

Doing the right work is both about examining the work of the business and the tasks you'll do personally in executing on that work. These two aspects of work are different and both are critically important.

The work of the business is the offer you deliver. Examples include comprehensive financial planning, investment management or more specialized work such as divorce or cross-border planning. Sixty-five percent of the Absolutely Engaged have defined and are living their ideal with respect to the work the firm does for clients; they focus almost exclusively on that work.

The work of the leader is a different thing and reflects the role that you play in delivering your offer. You might work directly with clients and focus on building relationships. Or you might take on a more strategic role and build a team that works with clients. Or, you might work with a select group of clients, perhaps those with more complex needs, and leave the rest of your team to manage the other clients. If you work in a smaller business, there's less likely to be a differentiation between the work of the business and the work of the leader. Sixty-eight percent of the Absolutely Engaged have defined and are living their ideal as it relates to the role they play on the team.

Your Offer

The reality is that, today, you may have a real passion for a particular type of work, but only do that work for a small percentage of your clients. If you're lucky, the clients who want to work with you also want the work that you love to do. But if that isn't the case, you probably don't force the issue, not if you're like the majority of advisors. Rather than telling the world that you provide a defined offer, it's easier to let clients dictate what that offer will be.

But what if you turned that around? What if you only did exactly the kind of work you loved to do? What would that look like?

In order to examine the work you should be doing, ask yourself a simple question.

When was the last time you were completely energized by the work you were doing? What characterized that work?

You might want to close your eyes for a moment and just go back to a time when you felt that time passed quickly while you were working, when you felt challenged but fulfilled. When you think about those times, what defined the work you were doing? Was it:

- The scope of the work (e.g., comprehensive financial planning or a more narrow focus on a specialization)

- The specific client situation (e.g., helping a client through a major life transition such as a divorce)

- The client need you were tackling (e.g., working with families across generations)

Your Role

Now, if it's relevant, ask yourself about the role you should play. If you're a one-man band right now, this question may not apply. Nevertheless, I believe it's important to think about the role you want to play in the future. That role may actually dictate how you structure your team and business today.

The reality is that on any given day you wear many hats. At the best times, you're playing the role you were meant to play, building your business and tapping into all of your talents. At other times you may be fiddling with the photocopier. In between you probably find yourself doing meaningful work that may or may not be exactly the work you should be doing to advance the business—work that needs to be done, just not necessarily by you. These activities might include things like entering data in a financial planning software or setting up meetings.

What if you spent the majority of your time doing the kind of work that helped to drive the business forward? What would it mean for you—and what would it mean for the business? In order to understand the role you should play, ask yourself this question:

How do you add the greatest value to this business? Put another way, what are the things that you, and you alone, should be doing to propel the business forward?

Take a moment and think about the activities that have the biggest impact in meeting your goals. We can't assume it's meeting with clients (although that might be the case) because this depends very much on your skills. For example, does the business grow when you focus your time on:

- Complex technical work
- Educating clients and prospects
- Acting as a rainmaker
- Working directly with clients
- Acting as the visionary

You may notice that when you thought about the times when you were doing the work you love, or you were with the clients with whom you love to work, time seemed to fly by. It's not an illusion; you were likely experiencing something called "flow.[11]" Flow is a metric that's often used with professional athletes as a measure of efficiency—when they get "in the zone." When you're focused on an activity, when you feel confident, when you've mastered the skill and when you're still suitably challenged, you perform at a higher level.

The connection to Absolute Engagement is clear. When you experience flow you create momentum, which is tied both to growth and fulfillment. Flow is tied to mastery, challenge, confidence and joy. It's active, which is why we rarely feel flow when we're sitting in front of the television at night. It also explains why we're less likely to experience flow when we've been doing the same thing in our business for too long. When you intentionally build your business around your passions, flow is triggered because you set clear goals and you stretch yourself relative to your existing skills.

Work: The Location

As an aside, the Absolutely Engaged were also much more likely to say that their work environment matched their ideal. Seventy percent had defined and were living their ideal in this area compared with 26 percent of all others.

I investigated this issue for very personal reasons. On my own journey I realized that it was important to me to be able to work from a home office or from anywhere in the world. That realization impacted the kind of work that I do and the kind of people I hire. I have purposely focused on work that can largely be executed from a computer anywhere in the world. As a test of the plan, my family and I travelled to Italy and spent a month there. The business was new and I had no team but kept things running from there without a hiccup. And while you may not be able to move around in the same way (or even care about it), it's worth asking yourself where you want to be when you're working.

Beware the Traps

As you dig deep and think about what you most enjoy, beware of two traps because you are, after all, human.

1. Self-Editing

This chapter is all about what's possible and I've purposefully asked you to think about what you love separately from how you might make it happen (the No-Decision Zone). The separation is difficult for many of us, who want to leap past the dream stage and focus on implementation. The problem is that when we do that we're prone to destructive self-editing.

Self-editing sounds a little like this.

"I love working with small business owners. I understand them and I know I can make a difference. More than that, they inspire me to do more with my own business. Wouldn't it be cool if my entire business was built around working with business owners? <Slight pause.> But, that would mean I might have to say "no" to some prospects and that could have an impact on revenue this year. And I did promise the kids I would take them

to Disney, so that's a problem. Plus, *some of my existing clients might not like it.* And, *Mary has been on my team for years and she doesn't really warm to business owners. Ah well, things are probably fine as they are."*

Dream = squashed. We're very good at editing ourselves out of taking action on a dream before we even take the first step.

2. The Endowment Effect

Another way we (perhaps unconsciously) give ourselves permission to continue with the status quo is the Endowment Effect[12]. The Endowment Effect leads us to ascribe more value to what we already have and less to what we may have in future. Put another way, once we're invested, we're committed.

If you've ever watched the television show *Shark Tank*, you'll see this in action. Entrepreneurs routinely ascribe a value to their businesses that's equal to the amount of time and money they have personally invested. They find out relatively quickly that the value may be zero until they can translate that investment into real revenue. In a similar way, sometimes we see our current business and path as more valuable than the alternative (the pursuit of Absolute Engagement) simply because we've invested so much of ourselves to where we are.

You Won't (Necessarily) Change Everything

While I'm talking about crafting a vision for your life and your business and about having the courage to change, I don't want to suggest that the outcome of this vision requires dramatic change. You probably won't go through this process and realize you really want to become a yoga instructor; rather you'll begin to see what you love to do in your existing business life.

However, by way of warning, the process can lead you in a very different direction.

- Rita Robbins is the president of Affiliated Advisors. She paused one day to ask how she could do something that would feed her creativity and passion while continuing to run her business. She bought a lavender farm—one of the largest commercial lavender farms in east Mississippi—that had seen better days. It needed a hefty dose of tender loving care and a business overhaul. Quite a stretch for a woman who lives in Manhattan and had never even had a backyard!

- After 25 years as a respected personal finance expert, Jason Butler paused and realized that he was driven and energized by inspiring, motivating and empowering people. He sold his share in the successful wealth management business he had founded and began to build a career as a speaker, an author and a start-up investor.

On a personal note, I went through this process as well. I had invested years of my life developing products and programs to support financial advisors in driving deeper client engagement. After some deep reflection, however, it became clear to me that I wanted to focus my energies on speaking and writing. I thought long and hard about the work that got me jumping out of bed in the morning, in contrast with the work that seemed to create a knot in my stomach.

What was unexpected in this process, however, was the realization that I wanted to do something I didn't feel fully equipped to do. Sometimes this process will push you to make changes that are fundamentally uncomfortable because you know you have work to do, that you'll need to improve, to be truly successful. In my case this meant devoting significant time and energy to becoming the kind of speaker I always wanted to be.

It's Decision Time

As you complete this first brainstorming step, you'll arrive at the first major crossroads. Your decision is this:

What will you do with this information? Now that you've clarified what you're passionate about, irrespective of whether that reflects your business today, will you use those insights to shape or refine your business vision? Or, will you set those insights aside, promising to come back to them later when you have more time.

In the next chapter we'll look at what it means to translate all of this into a meaningful business vision.

The Recap

- Awareness is about getting real on what matters, what you want and how you prioritize those things. This is where possibility lives.

- Awareness is difficult because it opens up the possibility of failure, feels selfish and requires extraordinary vision.

- Those who are Absolutely Engaged have answered three questions related to work, clients and role:

  ° Which clients do I most enjoy working with and what is common among those individuals?

  ° When was the last time I was completely energized by the work I was doing and what characterized that work?

  ° What are the things that I, and I alone, should be doing to propel the business forward?

- When you're doing the work that energizes and inspires you, you achieve "flow," which propels you forward.

- To achieve Absolute Engagement you need to be wary of two traps: self-editing your goals before you get a chance to start pursuing them and ascribing too much value to what you have today.

- You must decide if you'll use the insights you gain from this step to inform your business going forward, or push those feelings to the side and slip back into your comfort zone.

Your Turn

This is a tough one. Your goal with this step is to identify the components of a meaningful personal vision based on a deeper understanding of what energizes and inspires you. Take some time to consider the components of your personal vision for the future.

Download the full workbook at www.absoluteengagement.com/book and enter the code 'IfNotNow'. The workbook includes room to respond and tips to interpret your answers.

As it relates to your clients, with which 10 clients do you most enjoy working and what is common among those individuals?

_____
_____
_____
_____
_____
_____
_____
_____
_____
_____

As it relates to your offer, when was the last time you were completely energized by the work you were doing? What characterized that work?

_____
_____
_____
_____
_____
_____
_____
_____
_____

AWARENESS: THIS IS WHERE POSSIBILITY LIVES.

As it relates to your role, what are the things that you, and you alone, should be doing to propel the business forward?

_____

_____

_____

_____

_____

_____

_____

_____

_____

Based on your responses above, how would you describe the changes you want to see in your business? Select the changes that apply and leave those blank that you don't want to change or are not priorities.

○ I want to focus my business on the kind of work I truly love to do.

○ I want to focus my time on a more defined set of tasks or responsibilities.

○ I want to focus my business on a defined target group.

These changes define your personal vision and will be the focus of your work going forward.

As you worked through this step, were there questions that emerged or additional thinking that you want to do? Make note of that now so you can come back to that as you progress.

_____

_____

_____

_____

_____

YOUR PATH TO ABSOLUTE ENGAGEMENT

3 PRINCIPLES

1 Personal vision drives business vision.

2 Your client and team experience should be tailored to actively support your business vision.

3 You're human. Don't forget it.

YOUR COMFORT ZONE

ABSOLUTE ENGAGEMENT

STEP 1
AWARENESS
Create a personal vision based on a deeper understanding of what energizes and inspires you.

THE DECISION
Will you use that information to shape or refine your business vision?

IF NO — IF YES

STEP 2
AUDACITY
Translate your personal vision into a business vision by formalizing your target client, your offer and the role you will play on the team.

THE DECISION
Will you draw a line in the sand and say to the world that you deliver a defined offer to a defined target client?

IF NO — IF YES

STEP 3
ACTION
Design client and team experiences that are specifically tailored to reflect your business vision

THE DECISION
Will you change or update how you engage with clients and how you hire, retain and develop to reflect the needs of your target audience?

IF NO — IF YES

STEP 4
ACCOUNTABILITY
Create a structure that will give you the support you need to put your plan in place.

THE DECISION
Will you formalize a process of connecting with peers who will support and push you to succeed?

IF NO — IF YES

STEP 5
RENEWAL
Set intentional goals that support energy and creativity.

THE DECISION
Will you set specific, intentional goals for personal renewal?

IF NO — IIF YES

Complete the steps and you'll be at the intersection of financial success and personal fulfillment. The Absolutely Engaged report higher revenue, less stress, better health and more time spent doing the work they love.

5
AUDACITY:
THIS IS WHERE
COURAGE LIVES

STARTING POINT:
You have a personal
vision regarding the
clients, work and role
that energize and
inspire you.

THE NEXT STEP:
Translate your personal
vision into a business vision
by formalizing your target
client, your offer and the
role you'll play on the team.

Audacity is about translating your personal vision into a business vision. It's about using the insights you gleaned in the first step to formalize your target client, your offer and the role you'll play on the team. I've observed that those who are Absolutely Engaged draw a line in the sand and tell the world they deal with a defined group of clients and provide a defined offer. They're not all things to all people because their business vision is driven by the personal vision, which creates a natural focus.

This is where courage lives because it means accepting that going in a new direction may make you unappealing to some prospective clients. We all want to be loved by everyone, right? Keep in mind, however, that becoming more specific about what you do will make you dramatically more appealing to members of your target group. You'll become a magnet for the right clients. This step also takes courage because it requires that you let go of the business you "think" you should run and the person you "think" you should be in favor of being completely authentic.

Let's get to work translating all the self-reflection from the last chapter into a meaningful business vision. It's important to say that while I asked you to reflect on clients, work and role you may not want or need to make changes in all three areas. You may want to provide the offer you have today to a more defined target group or focus on different work for your existing target market. You may be playing exactly the right role on the team today or want that to change. As you work through the process, on the path to Absolute Engagement, keep those priorities in mind.

Clients

In the last chapter I asked you to open your mind and think about the clients with whom you most love to work. And rather than asking you a general question, I asked you to identify 10 clients with whom you love working and think about what they had in common. Sometimes awareness has to emerge; it might not always be obvious going into the process. In fact, it probably will take a while to figure this all out—if it were easy, everyone would have already done it! Recall, however, that core to the definition of Absolute Engagement is working with the *right* clients.

Let's take that information and make it more specific to how you'll define your target and ideal client by answering three questions:

1. Who is your target client?

Example: I want to work with women.

2. How can you narrow your target to a meaningful segment?

Example: I want to work with female business owners.

3. What are the characteristics of your ideal client?

Example: I want to work with female business owners who are optimistic, open to advice, take a long-term view and want to create a comprehensive financial plan.

....

Chris Moynes is a managing partner at One Sports+Entertainment Group. He works exclusively with professional athletes. And while it might be easy to assume this came naturally or that he was someone born with connections into that world, nothing could be further from the truth. After working as a financial advisor for many years, Chris realized that he loved to work with athletes (and particularly hockey players). It was a huge risk but he made the leap and redefined his positioning, his offer and his client acceptance criteria. At the time he had only three clients who were professional athletes so this meant starting over. It took a lot of time to build the business with this target, but he was true to his vision. And it worked. It took him 18 months to get back to the level of income he was at prior to making the change and has achieved significant growth since then.

....

Mark McNulty is the president of McNulty Group, a firm started by his father Barry McNulty. When Mark joined the firm, his father was focused on providing financial planning for independent professionals. The two sat down and reviewed the business to really understand where they were having the greatest impact on their clients' lives. One such area was providing dentists with in-depth advice on the management, structure and sale of their practices. On that basis it became clear that they could have a much greater impact by integrating the practice and personal planning of this group of clients. They began to focus solely on the dentist market and more specifically the baby boomer dentist. Today, the firm works only with that target and enjoys a leading position in that community.

....

Working With Multiple Target Markets

One of the questions that might strike you relates to my suggestion that you define a single target market. It's entirely possible that your passion pushes you in more than one direction (although sometimes we do that to avoid potentially difficult decisions). The challenge with multiple target markets is ensuring that prospective clients can clearly understand where they belong. To that end, I'd suggest three things need to be in place if you feel strongly that you need more than one target market.

- **Scale.** It takes an extraordinary amount of time and energy to truly meet the needs of a defined target market. For that reason, only firms with true scale have a chance of being successful in working with more than one. If you can create separate and defined teams, processes and offers for different target markets, then success is within your reach.

- **Alignment.** If you have the scale to effectively work with more than one target, then I'd suggest that those markets need to be aligned in some way. It would be confusing to see that you work with professional athletes and teachers, for example. However, you might focus on women and then drive that down to female business owners and female corporate executives.

- **Exclusivity.** I've had the experience of reading the descriptions of an advisor's target markets and feeling I belonged in all of them. I was confused and stuck. Don't make your clients work too hard to figure out which path they should pursue because they meet the criteria of all target markets.

Just Say No

We know that those who are Absolutely Engaged are twice as likely to have a clear definition of their ideal client. More important, however, they have learned how to say no. This means they are *living* their ideal, which is the second component in identifying those who are Absolutely Engaged.

The next chart highlights an important fact. More than half (51 percent) of those who are Absolutely Engaged say that three quarters of their clients fit their definition of the ideal. That drops off a cliff to just 17 percent of all others

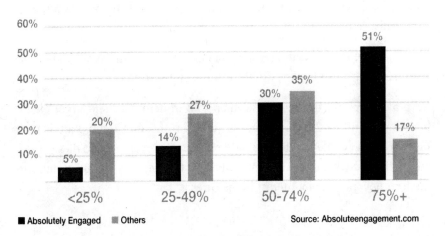

■ Absolutely Engaged ▨ Others   Source: Absoluteengagement.com

Q: What percentage of your clients would you say meet your definition of the ideal client?

I'm asking you to draw that line and begin to focus your business on this target and ideal client. Others have done it very successfully. **This is part one of your business vision.**

WORK: Your Offer

In the last chapter I asked you to think about the work that you love to do. And just as you did with clients, you'll want to translate that thinking into a defined offer, one that's specific enough to feed your passion. To that end, imagine how you would respond to the following two questions, focusing on that ideal work you want to deliver.

1. How would you describe the work you want to deliver to your clients?

• Example: I want to provide comprehensive financial planning to facilitate the efficient transfer of wealth from one generation to the next.

2. Can you restate that description (if needed) in a way that captures your ideal offer but in terms a client would understand? (Hint: Think about how you might describe the work that you do on your website or if you met a prospective client.)

- Example: I work with families to help them create a shared vision for wealth that will be supported by the next generation.

Several successful firms are less interested in defining their target client but are clear about the work that they do. The unstated assumption is that the work will be relevant for the right people, however, even in these cases they will identify the ideal client criteria so that there is a good match for the firm beyond just an interest in the offer.

....

Jon Jones is the co-CEO of Brighton Jones in Seattle. He has always had a charitable bent that influenced him personally. As the business grew, he translated this personal passion into a defined offer. His goal is to provide legacy planning for clients, which incorporates both philanthropic giving and working with the next generation. His firm not only provides financial planning but actively supports clients in supporting charities. In addition to the planning components, they feature local and international charities at client events, build team activities around giving back to the community and help to educate clients on charitable opportunities. In the process Jon has translated a personal vision into a defined offer for clients and then supported that throughout the organization.

....

Jennifer is a successful financial advisor in Virginia. She spent years building her career at a large financial institution but knew that there was a friction she had not fully addressed: She felt an inherent conflict between the work she wanted to provide (comprehensive financial planning) and the limitations imposed by her firm. She made the decision to leave her firm and start again in order to execute on her personal vision to help clients define a vision for their future and to help them establish meaningful legacies. There was risk and almost certain negative financial impact in the short term. She knew, however, that she wanted and needed to work with clients in a certain way and transformed her offer around comprehensive planning for families.

. . . .

As you think about how you will define your offer, remember to think about your why. If you could focus all or most of your time on the work you find most fulfilling, what would it mean to you, your business, your team and your clients?

I'm asking you to draw that line and begin to focus your business on this offer. Others have done it very successfully. **If this is part of what's important to you, then this is part two of your business vision.**

WORK: Your Role

In the last chapter, I also asked you to think about your role in delivering on the work of the business. There's a good chance it's a role that you play today (at least for part of your time) but thinking about what drives the business forward may have caused you to think about how you could re-structure your role. To create clarity in this area, think back to how you answered the questions on role in the last chapter and get more specific.

1. How would you define the role you want to play?

Example: I'd like to drive the strategy, brand and marketing for the firm.

2. What percentage of your time do you spend on this role today?

- Example: On average, I put 20% of my time into strategic marketing activities.

3. What would have to happen to allow you to spend more time on this role?

- Example: I'd have to transition responsibility for my clients to another senior advisor on the team, hire a paraplanner to allow the other advisor to manage more relationships, delegate administrative tasks, and work from home one day a week to create a quiet space to create content.

As an advisor you might believe that your one best role is providing advice to clients. It's a natural connection to make but it's not always the case. You may find that you can have a more meaningful impact by focusing on other aspects of the business. *Or* perhaps you do provide advice, but limit that to a select group of clients where you can make the most difference and the work reflects what really gets your juices flowing.

....

Jack Thurman is the managing partner of BKD Wealth Advisors, headquartered in Springfield, Missouri, with nine offices in the Central U.S. The firm is a subsidiary of BKD, LLP (a CPA and advisory firm). Jack was recruited to build and run the wealth management group within the larger organization. At the time the client base was small and comprised of clients that had been developed prior to Jack's arrival. Despite his background as an advisor, Jack did not work in the business as an advisor. He was a passionate visionary and when he was left to do that kind of work, to think about the future of the firm, to expand and to focus on culture, the business grew. In this case the way the financial advisor could build the business was not to be a financial advisor.

....

Kevan Herod is a partner with Herod Financial Services. He had grown a successful business and he knew it was time to evaluate the path forward. Going into the process it was assumed that the focus would be on how to standardize the client experience to create greater efficiency. It quickly became apparent, however, that in order to do that, he needed to define what the firm stood for and, by association, their target client. They landed on a plan that focused on legacy—both legacy as it related to the community and to charity. There was another layer to the story, however. As much as that was the focus that made sense, Kevan knew that his passion wasn't to work with all clients on delivering that work but a select group of clients with the most sophisticated needs. It was clear that the "work" of the business and the "work" of the founder needed to be defined and were not necessarily the same. Kevan's expertise supported the business best when he could focus his energies on these clients and that meant ensuring that the team was more actively involved with the other clients.

Once again, as you complete this section remember to think about your why. If you could focus all or most of your time on these activities what would it mean to you, your business, your team and your clients?

I'm asking you to draw that line and begin to focus your role. Others have done it very successfully. **If this is part of what's important to you, then this is part three of your business vision.**

What Changes Will You Make?

At this point you've thought about the target audience with whom you'll work and the work you want to provide (as a business or personally). Your business vision should be clear and comprise the specific areas that were most important to you. It might also be daunting but I'm hoping you can live with that as we move forward! If the work you've just done uncovers changes in multiple areas (e.g., you want to change clients, work and role), you'll need to prioritize so that you can manage the process and keep your sanity.

The order in which you take action should be driven primarily by what is most important to you. Don't try and turn your entire world upside down overnight; this should be a staged and thoughtful process. I'd recommend changing your clients, offer or both before changing your role, as you'll need to be actively involved in the process. However, if the role you've taken on doesn't provide you with a moment's time to make these changes, then delegation may be the first thing you need to do.

Putting the Plan to the Test

Now it's time to take a step back and make sure that the changes you want to make are not only manageable but represent real economic opportunity. While I'm asking you to stay focused on your passion, that's not to the exclusion of meaningful growth. You know that the target client and offer you've defined are meaningful to you based on the work you've already done. So you're left with two questions.

- Does the plan represent a significant economic opportunity and/or what will the economic impact be on your business in the short and longterm to make these changes?

- Will the plan be meaningful to prospective and existing clients?

Does the Plan Make Economic Sense?

At the risk of stating the obvious, your version of the ideal business needs to reflect a meaningful economic opportunity. That opportunity will be influenced by:

- the size of the potential market

- your access to that market

- the extent to which your business is built to effectively serve that market (more on that in the next step)

Let's look at two extreme examples to make the point. If your goal is to work with farmers you can be confident, intuitively, that there's a substantial market. If, however, you live in the middle of Manhattan, then access may be a problem. Take another example: You may want to focus on brain surgeons and have a full list of those medical professionals in your community. You have access. But if there are only three brain surgeons in your community, then the access won't matter—there's just not enough of a target market.

While you may not need to know the exact number of people in your target market (e.g., because it's obviously a sizable market), you'll want to do some analysis on the impact on your existing business. Your long-term goal will, or should, be to transition to an exclusive (or near-exclusive) focus on your target market and offer, but you'll need to make some decisions as to how you make that happen.

To get a handle on the impact, ask yourself the following questions.

• What proportion of my clients is part of my ideal target market?

• For what proportion of clients do I currently provide my ideal offer?

• What proportion of my clients is in my target market and receive my ideal offer?

Based on your answers above, examine the potential economic impact of each of the following three scenarios:

1. What would the impact be if I transferred out any client who does not fit within my ideal target immediately? This is a straight calculation of the assets represented by clients who don't fit today.

2. What would the impact be if I kept my existing client base but only accepted new clients who are part of my ideal target? This is an estimate of the growth you might expect if you focused all your attention on attracting your target market. You may also want to factor in some attrition among existing clients who don't fit within your target.

3. What would the impact be if I transferred clients who don't fit over time and only accepted new clients who are part of my ideal target? This is an estimate of the length of time it would take to complete the transition if you transferred clients out at roughly the same rate as you attracted new clients.

Your decision is an important one. In the next chapter I'll be asking you to structure your business around the needs of your target. That has certain implications if you plan on keeping existing clients who are not part of your target. For example, how will existing clients feel if you begin to change your communications or process to fit the needs of a different target? You need to address the issue but I hope you fight the urge to water down your communications to appeal to everyone (and no one).

Will the Plan be Meaningful to Your Clients?

Perhaps the bigger test is the one that determines if the target market and offer you have defined will be meaningful to clients and prospects. I truly believe that if you have chosen a market based on an authentic assessment of your own passions, you'll be on the right path. If, however, you've chosen a target market because you think it might be a big market or because it's a common market, it may not pass the authenticity test. And authenticity matters when it comes to your offer and your target audience. This is why it's so important to do you your inner work first, and then move into the external work.

To test if the plan is meaningful consider a trial balloon and the authenticity test.

Trial Balloon

You might want to reach out to a handful of existing clients and float the idea of a new focus for your business. This is a helpful process to ensure that you're on the right path. Start by selecting a few clients who are in your new, ideal target market and ask if you can get their input. Try this on for size:

I love working with <insert ideal client here>, just like you. It turns out that I'm already working with a number of clients who fall into this category. I'm thinking of making some significant changes to my business *so that I can focus all of my attention on meeting the needs of this target audience. Specifically, that would mean that when I send out articles, they'll be targeted to these clients and the same holds for workshops we run. And we'll be adding services and expertise that are targeted to this kind of client.*

Then get their reaction. Would they find it appealing? Why? Would it increase your perceived value? Would it make you easier to refer? I don't recommend that you ask if they would be more inclined to work with you if you focused exclusively on people like them. Because clients have a relationship with you already, this is too difficult to answer because they can't go back in time to the point when they didn't have a relationship with you. It's a bit like asking if you would have preferred to have had a child with athletic ability; you might like the idea but you're clearly committed to your existing children.

The Authenticity Test

One of the best ways to assess if the target and offer you have chosen is the right one, is something I call the Authenticity Test. Imagine you have a blank white board in front of you. On that white board you're going to describe the clients you consider to be ideal. It's a blank slate —it doesn't need to reflect your business today but what you want to create.

Complete this sentence:

At <your firm name>, we work with clients who.....

What words did you use to define that ideal client for your business? Were they the same as you mapped out earlier in this chapter or did you refine it when it was in the form of this kind of sentence? Now imagine that white board was a welcome sign to your office and I was the prospect. That description not only has to reflect what you care about, but it has to compel me to walk through the door.

Now it starts to get interesting. So often in our industry we see target markets that are some version of the following:

- We work with clients who are pre-retirees and have $250,000 or more in total investable assets.

- We work with wealthy families to help them transfer wealth to the next generation in a tax-efficient manner.

Now I have to ask. If your target is defined only by age and wealth, does that really inspire you? Does it get your heart racing a little faster? Perhaps it does, but I'm guessing that isn't the case. And, just as important, think about how that definition looks on your welcome sign. If I read that you work with pre-retirees on your door, am I bounding through? Do I feel inspired? Do I feel like you understand who I am and what I need? Of course not.

So authenticity plays an important role here. To test authenticity, imagine there's a second part to that sign. Now it says:

At <your firm name> we work with clients who... .

The reason we work with those clients is because... .

When you say it out loud you'll know if it's a hit or a miss. Was that full description compelling? Was it authentic? Would it be meaningful to both you and the prospective client? Would your existing clients relate to the description?

....

Randy Gerber is the founder of Gerber, LLC, in Columbus. He always enjoyed working with business owners and he recognized that their needs went far beyond investment management. In particular he recognized that perhaps more than any other group, there was a melding of business and life that had to be managed to help them live the best lives possible. But it wasn't just business owners that inspired him, it was first-generation business owners—those who were the founders and creators of their businesses and wealth, rather than the managers or stewards of those businesses and wealth in a later generation. Over a long period of time, he refocused his business to work exclusively with first-generation business owners and it's authentic.

When you go to Randy's homepage, here's what you see.

Why do we work with first-generation business owners? Because our founder believes that they are the world's creators...

....

In that single sentence, Randy tells the world who he works with, he acknowledges that he has a deep respect for those individuals and he compels his target audience to work with him. Hold that up against another site that simply says "we can work with business owners" and you get the point.

In fairness, if you're focused on pre-retirees in a very authentic way then there's nothing wrong with that. However, you'll still need to communicate the why. For example, you might say something like this. "I work exclusively with clients who are within five years of retirement. Research has shown clearly that too high a percentage of people aren't fully prepared to retire, not only based on their investments but because they haven't defined a meaningful vision for their lives when they stop working. As a result, too many people aren't living out their retirements with purpose and focus. I'm passionate about helping my clients create a vision that is inspiring and then take the steps they need to take to make it happen."

Now let's try the same exercise with your offer.

At <your firm name> we work with clients who....

The reason we work with those clients is because....

We provide.....

The reason we provide this is because....

When you say all of that out loud does it sound authentic? Does it get you excited for the future? Can you imagine your team rallying around this focus? Can you picture the prospect opening that door, picking up the phone or clicking on the '"contact us" button on your website based on that definition?

If not, ask yourself "why" again and again until you get to the true basis of your affinity for a certain type of client or work. This is a technique that journalists use. They just keep asking why until they get an answer that rings true. It may be frustrating as all get-out, but it works. Give yourself time—and keep asking. You'll get there!

Communicate Your Why

In many respects this exercise mirrors some of what author Simon Sinek talks about in his wonderful book *Start With Why*[13]. Sinek is an influential thinker and the author of three books. He talks about articulating your *why* as opposed to your *what*, which is what most firms spend a lot of time articulating. He goes on to say that your *why* isn't about making money—that's actually your result. He encourages you to understand *why* your company exists and why anyone should care. The authenticity test I just suggested is one way to not only force yourself to articulate your why, but also to assess whether you've nailed it.

One of the greatest marketing pieces you'll ever write is one that articulates your why for your target audience. Once you've completed the work in this chapter and you have a clear statement of your *why*, document it. Your document might take the form of an article, a blogpost or video—anything that clearly articulates why you do what you do. Next, share that message with prospects to set you apart and help them understand what working with you is all about. That might mean you:

- Write a blogpost

- Put a letter on your website

- Send an email to your clients

- Send your letter to prospects before you meet

- Share your letter with your centers of influence

- Or, all of the above

Why Does Focus Matter So Much?

Audacity is a complex step on the path to Absolute Engagement. I'm asking you to draw a line in the sand and focus your business. There's no doubt that as you worked through this process, you asked yourself some obvious questions.

- If I focus all my efforts on one group of clients or too narrowly define my offer, won't I miss out on some opportunities?

- If things are going well now, why would I want to change?

Well, the reality is that change matters. Change means growth, evolution, learning and passion. It matters if your goal is Absolute Engagement and it matters for three very specific reasons:

1. Intrinsic Motivation

You're the greatest catalyst for growth in your business. The problem is, you're human. If you feel passionate about the target and the offer, it will provide the motivation that you need every day to keep things moving. Your natural motivation will push you to succeed because you'll be energized and inspired, and not only because you are trying to hit a revenue goal (although that's a likely outcome as well). Those who are Absolutely Engaged are more passionate about the work they are doing. Ninety-six percent of this group indicated they "completely agree" that they're passionate about their work, compared with 76 percent of all others.

2. Law of Diffusion

If you're like most advisors, a quick scan of your client base will uncover a heterogeneous group. You may have set a revenue or asset minimum, but your clients' needs are likely to be diverse simply because of who they are. You might work with some business owners, a few doctors, an engineer or two, a number of corporate executives and a large number of folks who've already retired. The only obvious thing they have in common is working with you.

You sit at the center of this diverse group with the singular goal of adding significant value for all of them. As a result of that laudable goal, you are virtually pulled in a hundred directions, honestly trying to add value to everyone.

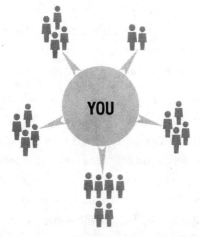

What if, instead, all of your energies were focused on finding solutions for—adding value to—the lives of clients who had similar needs and aspirations? What would that mean to your efficiency and expertise? And what would it mean to your own level of fulfillment?

Delivering on an extraordinary client experience means you know and understand the problems, lives and challenges of your clients better than anyone else. The reality is, however, that diverse needs diffuse your effort. By trying to engage everyone, you engage no one. And while that won't necessarily lead to client dissatisfaction, it may limit your chances for true client engagement.

3. Differentiation

When you've built a business around the needs of a clearly defined target audience, you quite simply become a magnet for the right clients. You're clearly differentiated from everyone else for just that reason. As a result, the right clients find you and this drives growth.

It's not hard to see how this happens. Imagine, for example, that a prospective entrepreneur client has been referred to two different advisors. He or she jumps online to get to know the firms before reaching out. Both are credible, reputable firms and both provide the services that the prospect would need. The prospect goes first to LinkedIn to find profiles for the two advisors. They both list the professional associations with which they work, but one also lists membership in "A Startup Specialists Group—an Online Network for Entrepreneurs" as well as "Startups and Bright Ideas & Entrepreneurs."

Next the prospect goes to Facebook and finds corporate pages for both advisors. Both share information about their businesses and team, but one includes links to the 10 best Facebook pages for entrepreneurs. Finally, the prospect goes to the websites, each of which are well-designed and provide information on the services the advisor provides. On the homepage of one, the advisor talks about helping clients build and transfer wealth and on the other it talks about the connection that entrepreneurs have between their businesses and their lives and the ways in which that creates unique challenges when it comes to planning for retirement. As an entrepreneur that prospect feels like they're home on the second site and everything he or she read and saw led to that point as if drawn there by a magnet.

We've covered a lot of ground and I hope I've managed to convince you that creating a clear business vision based on your personal vision is the best next step. Recall that the advisors who were Absolutely Engaged—who had achieved all the professional and personal benefits we outlined earlier—had defined and were living their ideal as it related to clients, work and role. While taking action might seem daunting, it is quite literally at the core of Absolute Engagement.

The Decision

As you complete step two, you'll come to the second major crossroads. Your decision is this:

Will you draw a line in the sand and say to the world that you deliver a defined offer to a defined target client? Or, will you continue as you are, trying to do all of the right things for everyone (or no one)?

In the next chapter we'll look at what it means to bring your refreshed business vision to life. Hold on tight, there's more work to be done.

The Recap

- Audacity is about translating your personal vision into a business vision. It's about using the insights you gleaned in the "awareness phase" to formalize your target client, your offer and the role you will play on the team. This is where courage lives.

- Take action by translating your thinking and brainstorming about clients into a clear definition of your target and ideal client. Then, clearly define your offer and the role you will play in delivering on that offer.

Continued on the next page

- To drive action, define the impact that the right clients, right work and right role will have on you, your business, your clients and your team.

- In order to assess your plan:

  ° Examine the economic opportunity and impact of making changes to your target, offer and role.

  ° Determine if your plan will resonate with your clients, authentically.

- Focusing on a clear target and offer has three primary benefits:

  ° It taps into your intrinsic motivation and passion.

  ° It focuses your efforts rather than diffusing them.

  ° It differentiates you from other advisors.

- You must decide if you'll draw a line in the sand and tell the world that you work with a defined target client to deliver a defined offer.

Your Turn

Your goal with this step is to translate your personal vision into a business vision by formalizing your target client, your offer and the role you will play on the team. Take some time to articulate these elements of your ideal business.

Download the full workbook at www.absoluteengagement.com/book and enter the code 'IfNotNow'. The workbook includes room to respond and tips to interpret your answers.

Your Clients

Describe your target client.

_____

_____

_____

_____

_____

Narrow your target to a meaningful segment.

_____

_____

_____

_____

Define the characteristics of your ideal client.

_____

_____

_____

_____

_____

How would working only with this type of client impact:
You?

_____
_____
_____
_____
_____

Your business?

_____
_____
_____
_____
_____

Your team?

_____
_____
_____
_____
_____

Your clients?

_____
_____
_____
_____
_____

Your Offer

Describe the work you want to deliver to your clients.

_____
_____
_____
_____

Re-state that description (if needed) in a way that captures your ideal offer in terms a client would understand. Think about how you might describe the work that you do on your website or if you met a prospective client.

_____
_____
_____
_____
_____

How would doing only this kind of work impact:
You?

_____
_____
_____
_____

Your business?

_____
_____
_____
_____

Your team?

_____
_____
_____
_____

Your clients?

_____
_____
_____

Your Role

What is the role you (and you alone) should play on the team?

_____

_____

_____

_____

_____

What percentage of your time do you spend on this role today? _____%

What would have to happen to allow you to spend more time on this role?

_____

_____

_____

_____

_____

How would focusing only on these activities impact:
You?

_____

_____

_____

_____

_____

Your business?

_____

_____

_____

_____

_____

Your team?

_____

_____

_____

_____

_____

Your clients?

_____

_____

_____

_____

_____

The Transition

Think about the following relative to your ideal target:

What proportion of your clients are part of your ideal
target market?   _____%

For what proportion of clients do you currently provide
your ideal offer?   _____%

What proportion of your clients are both in your target
and receive your ideal offer?   _____%

On the basis of that analysis, what is the best approach to take with the
following two groups?

Existing clients who do not fit into this definition of your ideal?

_____

_____

_____

_____

_____

THE PURSUIT OF ABSOLUTE ENGAGEMENT

New clients who do not fit into this definition of your ideal?

_____
_____
_____
_____
_____

Will you float the concept of a more targeted client or offer to your clients? If yes, how?

_____
_____
_____
_____
_____

Complete the following sentences relative to your target and offer
At my firm we work with clients who.....

_____
_____
_____
_____
_____

The reason we work with those clients is because....

_____
_____
_____
_____
_____

We provide.....

_____
_____
_____
_____

The reason we provide this is because....

_____

_____

_____

_____

_____

Now that you've translated your personal vision into a defined business vision, will you draw a line in the sand and say to the world that you deliver a defined offer to a defined target client?

◯ Yes, I'm continuing down the path to Absolute Engagement

◯ No, my comfort zone is looking good right now

What do you see as the potential barriers at this stage?

_____

_____

_____

_____

_____

What are the specific next steps you will take, based on what you have read in this chapter and written about your own business?

1. _____
2. _____
3. _____
4. _____
5. _____

PART THREE:
TAILORING
YOUR CLIENT AND
TEAM EXPERIENCE

Your client and team experience should be designed to both align with—and actively support—your business vision.

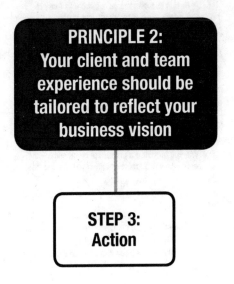

PRINCIPLE 2:
Your client and team experience should be tailored to reflect your business vision

STEP 3:
Action

YOUR PATH TO ABSOLUTE ENGAGEMENT

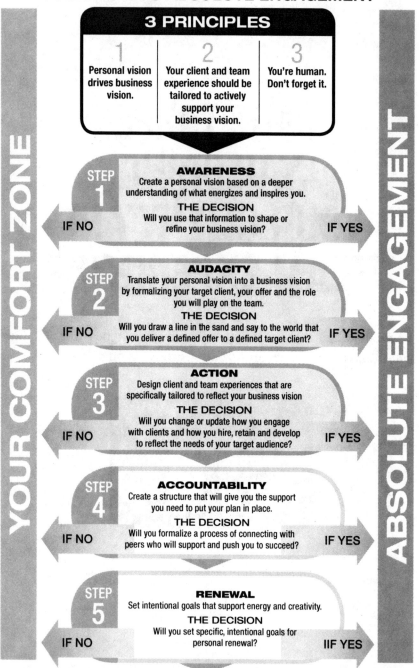

3 PRINCIPLES

1 Personal vision drives business vision.

2 Your client and team experience should be tailored to actively support your business vision.

3 You're human. Don't forget it.

YOUR COMFORT ZONE

ABSOLUTE ENGAGEMENT

STEP 1 — AWARENESS
Create a personal vision based on a deeper understanding of what energizes and inspires you.

THE DECISION
Will you use that information to shape or refine your business vision?

IF NO   IF YES

STEP 2 — AUDACITY
Translate your personal vision into a business vision by formalizing your target client, your offer and the role you will play on the team.

THE DECISION
Will you draw a line in the sand and say to the world that you deliver a defined offer to a defined target client?

IF NO   IF YES

STEP 3 — ACTION
Design client and team experiences that are specifically tailored to reflect your business vision

THE DECISION
Will you change or update how you engage with clients and how you hire, retain and develop to reflect the needs of your target audience?

IF NO   IF YES

STEP 4 — ACCOUNTABILITY
Create a structure that will give you the support you need to put your plan in place.

THE DECISION
Will you formalize a process of connecting with peers who will support and push you to succeed?

IF NO   IF YES

STEP 5 — RENEWAL
Set intentional goals that support energy and creativity.

THE DECISION
Will you set specific, intentional goals for personal renewal?

IF NO   IIF YES

Complete the steps and you'll be at the intersection of financial success and personal fulfillment. The Absolutely Engaged report higher revenue, less stress, better health and more time spent doing the work they love.

6
ACTION:
THIS IS WHERE
CONFIDENCE LIVES

STARTING POINT:
You've clarified your
ideal client and offer
in a way that reflects
your personal vision.

THE NEXT STEP:
Understand the trends that
will influence how to craft
an engaging client and team
experience.

At this point it's all about Action, about breathing life into the business vision you crafted in the last chapter. Action has three components. First and foremost, Action is about tailoring your client and team experience to specifically reflect your offer and the unique needs of your target market, while freeing you up to take on the role that will push the business forward. Second, it's about determining what role you'll play in the process and putting the structure in place to make that happen. Finally, it's about driving deeper relationships by creating engaging experiences for both your clients and your team. This is where confidence lives, because taking action demands that you analyze every aspect of how you deliver your service and question if that is fully aligned with your personal and business visions.

Taking action on your audacious goal will require change in how you run the business, so this step is about taking a focused and intentional approach to making those changes. If Audacity is about *what* you'll deliver and to whom then Action is about *how* you'll do it.

In examining the businesses of the Absolutely Engaged, you'll see an important concept reflected—perfect alignment between personal, client and team engagement. Put another way, personal vision drives the business vision and that business vision now needs to actively influence both your client and team experience. You don't address those components in isolation. Often we think about personal, client and team engagement separately. We define what we consider to be an extraordinary client experience and an extraordinary team experience but without necessarily asking how our personal and business visions should affect them.

If you try to define a client experience but haven't defined a clear target, for example, you end up creating something that is good but not great because it isn't created around the needs of your target audience. If your client experience is built to meet the needs of anyone, you water down the experience for everyone. Or you might focus a great deal of attention on trying to create a positive team environment in an effort to create loyalty. But think about this: The very team members you need to put in place will be influenced by your personal and business visions. As a result, how you nurture, develop and reward your team is also tied to that business vision.

In the three chapters that follow, we're going to do a deep dive on the process of defining your client experience, your role and your team experience, based on the inner work you've already completed. I'll look at approaches you can take and share some specific tactics and examples along the way.

What Drives Engagement?

As you progress, you'll not only focus on a tailored experience, but an engaging experience. So I thought we should take some time and examine what engagement really means and focus on three ideas:

- Satisfaction and loyalty are no longer enough.

- Engagement is the new standard.

- Engagement is being disrupted based on a shift from service to experience and the concept of co-created value.

1. Satisfaction and Loyalty Are No Longer Enough

It might be surprising that I'm suggesting that satisfaction and loyalty are no longer enough in the same breath as discussing a great client experience. The reality is that the two metrics we've traditionally used to measure success with both our clients and our teams—satisfaction and loyalty—don't set the bar high enough.

Let's start with a look at satisfaction and I'll use coffee as a good example. It's not uncommon for me to stop by a major coffee chain to pick up a highly overpriced cup of coffee as I head out to meetings. If I reflect on my last experience, it was pretty good. The coffee was exactly as I expected, it arrived quickly and my barrista was almost unnervingly friendly.

Now it strikes me that if some eager market researcher was waiting for me outside the door and asked me to rate my level of satisfaction, I would have rated it as very high. The coffee shop delivered exactly what I expected and did it well. But it also strikes me that, other than telling you about this experience, I will not share it with anyone else. Satisfaction, though important, is not worth sharing with friends and family. And if another chain with a similar offer opened up closer to home, I would probably jump ship in a heartbeat.

Which takes us to loyalty. There are fewer better examples of the loyalty dichotomy as the airlines. I have the bad luck to fly a lot for my work and I tend to fly the same airline. It strikes me that if the president of that airline decided to review the list of frequent flyers, on any given day, he might see my name and draw the conclusion that I love that airline. He would, I can assure you, be wrong. I'm loyal but not necessarily happy. I'm something of a hostage to airline points but it would be wrong to associate loyalty with the quality of the relationship. Loyalty alone isn't negative, but it certainly doesn't mean it's positive if clients simply don't feel there is a good alternative.

As much as satisfaction and loyalty are important—they are necessary but not sufficient conditions of a great or even a good relationship. What these experiences make clear is that by creating satisfaction and loyalty, neither the coffee company nor the airlines set themselves apart. The same is true for financial services. I see that in the data I collect from more than 1,000 investors every year. When I ask them about their relationship with their financial advisor the news is, perhaps contrary to media reports, quite positive.

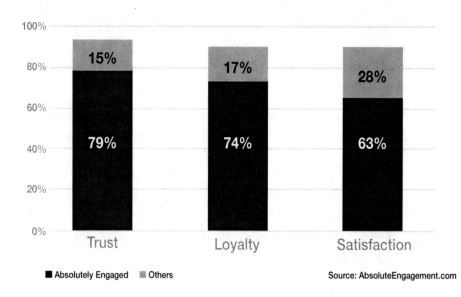

Q: Trust: To what extent do you agree or disagree that your financial advisor is trustworthy? (4 is somewhat agree, 5 is strongly agree)

Q: Loyalty: How likely are you to continue to use your financial advisor to manage your financial plan or portfolio in the next 12-24 months? (4 is somewhat likely, 5 is very likely)

Q: Satisfaction: Please rate your overall level of satisfaction with your financial advisor. (4 is somewhat satisfied, 5 is very satisfied)

This data should result in an industrywide pat on the back and an outburst of self- congratulation but you might notice something important about the pattern of the graph. When clients report almost universally good relationships, none of these metrics make an advisor distinctive. In fact, having satisfied clients makes an advisor just as good as everyone else, not better. Satisfaction and loyalty (and even trust) simply don't set you apart. So while you can create an experience that feels satisfying to your clients, it might not help you attract new clients or create the level of engagement you seek. I'd suggest that this same concept applies to teams. We can focus all of our energies on creating a satisfied and loyal team, but that falls short of creating a truly engaged team.

2. Engagement is the New Standard

With the view that satisfaction and loyalty are not enough, our research goes further to establish a rating that includes these two metrics but adds referrals and wallet share into the mix. We established a new standard— client engagement—that isolates the most satisfied clients, the most loyal clients and those who drive growth. These engaged clients not only help you grow and not only stick around for the long run, but also feel better about their relationship with you and are more confident in their own financial future. These are the clients who will be crucial to the health and growth of your business. About a quarter of clients are engaged so it's something of an aspirational standard, but I happen to think that's a good thing.

So if we accept that engagement is a better standard, it's important to understand the trends that might influence—or potentially disrupt—client engagement going forward.

Disrupter #1: From client service to client experience

First up is a shift from service to experience. In the past, when we talked about clients we focused on delivering "good service" and that, we believed, was enough to create a good relationship. Today we realize that good service is a relatively low bar—it means that the product or service was delivered in a manner that met expectations. I bought a coffee; I received a coffee. I hired an architect; the building was built.

Delivering good service—getting the fundamentals right—doesn't set you apart.

It's possible that we stick slavishly to the notion that client service sets us apart because we have a tendency to overstate what we actually deliver. You're probably familiar with the statistic that 90 percent of drivers perceive themselves as above average behind the wheel. I don't have to point out the mathematical impossibility of this statement. It seems that a similar overconfidence colors our view of our own client service. In a study of advisors from the Financial Planning Association[14], respondents were asked what differentiates them from other advisors. Seventy-two percent said it was their strong customer service. Again, it's almost impossible that nearly three quarters of advisors can stand out based on their strong service. There has to be something deeper, something more.

Here's a different way to look at things. In our investor research, we segment clients into four groups based on satisfaction, loyalty, wallet share and referral activity. We call those groups disgruntled, complacent, content and engaged. We then look at about 35 different aspects of service and examine the connection to engagement. What we find is a path from satisfaction to engagement defined by service, offer and leadership.

At the base of pyramid you see service. It's table stakes—it means that you must get the basics right. You're responsive, you don't make too many errors and you keep your clients up to date. If you don't deliver on this,

then you don't make it out of the gate and your clients will become disgruntled very quickly. Bear in mind, however, that picking up the phone just a little faster doesn't create a deeper or more engaged relationship.

The next level is offer, which reflects the work that you do for clients. The scope of the work is tied to client engagement. Specifically, we see a direct link between having a written financial plan and engagement. While I don't believe that you need to provide financial planning to engage clients, the data suggests that the more comprehensive the offer—the more it connects you to what's most important to your clients, their lives and their families—the more engaged those clients will be.

At the top of the pyramid you'll find leadership. Leadership is about the role that you play in the lives of your clients; when clients are engaged they tend to describe their advisor as a "leader." In our research we went deeper on exactly what that means and asked clients an open-ended question to define leadership. The data suggests that leadership is connected to three things: your expertise, the extent to which you fully understand the needs of your clients and the extent to which you proactively provide guidance. In fact, "guidance" was the No. 1 word used in this unaided question.

When I think about guidance, I think about you taking your client by the hand and pulling them through the process of defining a vision for their future and helping them to face the difficult decisions they need to make. Guidance, for example, is helping an entrepreneur see the importance of insurance because they're left without a safety net if they can't work for a period of time. It's about helping your clients communicate more effectively about money. It's about helping a client who has been "retired" due to downsizing to reinvent themselves. Guidance is about all the things that are critically important to the financial future of your clients, but which sometimes need a steady, guiding hand.

As you think about mapping out your client and team experience, think about how that experience demonstrates real leadership to your clients and to your team.

Disrupter #2: Co-Creation of Value

The next trend I see disrupting client engagement is a concept called "co-creation of value." The concept of co-creation of value has a credible analytical history going back to the seventies and is linked to researchers C.K. Prahalad and Venkat Ramaswamy[15]. In many cases the term is used to underscore the importance of client input in understanding value. However, I believe it goes further to reflect how clients can actively contribute to value creation and, therefore, engagement.

Simply stated, co-creation of value focuses on how you (or your firm) work with clients and your team to create value together. In the past, value was created "by" firms and offered "to" clients. That meant that the primary goal of the business was to identify and target the right clients for the product/service being made. In the future, according to this theory, value will be driven more by clients, who will take an active role in the innovation of the product, service and overall experience.

My own definition takes the form of a question. Instead of asking what can we *offer to* clients in order to drive engagement, we need to ask what we can *create with* clients in order to drive engagement.

To demonstrate how things have changed, let's look at three examples, going back to my cup of coffee at the start of this chapter.

- **In the beginning, there was firm-driven value.** For example, a coffee chain opens a shop on your corner. You can choose to buy the coffee that is available (or not).

- **Next came client-centric value.** For example, a coffee company crafts a range of coffees that reflects the tastes of several key client segments. You can choose the coffee best suited to you (or not).

- **Now we're moving toward co-created value.** For example, a coffee company creates an online forum in which clients influence product development, service offerings and the overall experience. As the client, you're invited to post comments and answer surveys— and now you're actively involved in the innovation and development of the entire experience. You're choosing to be involved as much as you are choosing to buy, creating a sense of ownership and identification with the result.

Co-creation and the shift to Client Involvement

I make no secret of the fact that I love client feedback as an engagement and growth tool. Yet while client feedback, as the coffee example makes clear, is a part of the co-creation of value, it has limitations. Traditional quantitative client feedback involves a survey of clients (typically online but also potentially executed by phone) in which clients are asked a set of questions and provided with a predefined set of responses. Perhaps the most significant limitation of this form of quantitative feedback is that it confines the scope of the response. In fact, your own assumptions and bias are likely to inform the possible responses, which have obvious faults.

As a result of those limitations, I'd suggest that quantitative surveys are a great way to help shape your thinking about client experience and, in particular, a great way to measure performance (more on this in Chapter 7 when we get into the client experience). However, co-creation of value requires more, and suggests that client feedback can be used in a very different way. Rather than asking clients to assess performance or rate satisfaction or interest, you will be using a more active form of feedback, which involves the client in the process of defining or refining your client experience.

Here are some companies that are getting creative about client involvement.

- **Starbucks.** The firm actively solicits consumer input that informs their products, services and the overall experience in their stores.

- **Lego.** The firm has created tools that allow customers to build whatever they want. Lego provides the building blocks but customers can use those to build something completely unique and personal. The company also invites consumers to suggest new Lego sets—and those suggestions that can garner 10,000 online votes go into production.

- **Fitbit.** The tool tracks your steps while inviting you to enter additional information about your health so that the outcome is greater than what the firm alone could provide.

At a minimum, this particular disrupter suggests that we need to invite clients into the conversation to help us define a great client experience.

Perhaps the bigger transformation promised by a co-created approach is the way in which clients experience working with you. There are two key questions that will be critical for anyone who wants to co-create the experience.

- **Are you creating an experience that supports two-way communication?** For example, are meeting agendas co-created so that you are focusing on what is most important to clients? Are you making effective use of technology to actively engage the client during a review meeting?

- **Are you personalizing the client experience?** This might involve asking clients what topics they're interested in learning about (e.g., Social Security or financial literacy) as well as how they want to receive that information (e.g., articles, workshops, webinars). Personalizing the client experience, in this example, would involve providing clients with the kind of education they want in the way they want to receive it.

While the examples above relate specifically to client experience, you can easily see how the same concepts will apply to team experience. With the team, your goal here is to:

- Achieve deep engagement with your team, rather than promoting an environment they find merely "satisfying."

- Create a team experience that actively engages team members by supporting them in meeting their most significant professional and personal goals. (They, too, are looking for leadership.)

- Involve the team in defining what an extraordinary team looks like— to co-create the experience.

When Do You Tell the Team?

While we're on the topic of the team, there's something we haven't yet addressed and that's when and how you tell them about your goal of achieving Absolute Engagement and the path to get there. The reality is that the order of operations can be a little fluid. There are elements of both the client and team experience that will be driven by you and those that will be co-created with the team. I recommend that you move fully through the Awareness and Audacity steps to gain a clear understanding of where you are going. At that point you'd be wise to bring the team together and share your vision for the future, inviting their input but remaining true to your goals.

When you share your vision with the team, by all means get all of their questions or concerns on the table. No doubt this will serve as a good exercise to ensure that you've thought your plans through from every angle. I think it's important, however, to recognize that you're asking for input and feedback at this point, and not co-creating the vision. As you're the owner and leader of the firm, the company vision needs to be a reflection of your personal vision.

Nevertheless, your team's active involvement will be critical in the next phase, which is all about tailoring and defining the client and team experience. You want and need their input, their buy-in and their support. Tell them about your plans too soon and you run the risk of questioning your own motivation. Tell them too late and you run the risk of alienating them and creating a substandard experience.

As you think about mapping out your client and team experience, think about how you can actively involve the client and your team to understand what a truly engaging experience looks like, through the client's eyes. With a clear idea of what's engaging in mind, you can turn to the client experience, your role and the team experience.

The Recap

- Action is about tailoring your client and team experience to specifically reflect your offer and the unique needs of your target, while freeing you up to take on the role that will push the business forward. This is where confidence lives.

- When there is alignment between personal, client and team engagement you create a form of momentum that propels the business forward.

- Satisfaction and loyalty are no longer enough. Achieving high ratings on these metrics makes you just as good as everyone else—but not distinctive.

- Engagement is the new standard. Engagement creates a fundamentally different, deeper and more connected relationship with your clients.

- Engagement is being disrupted by two trends:

  ° A shift from client service to client experience. Client service is table stakes but engagement is driven by the right offer and active leadership.

  ° Co-creation of value focuses on how you work with your clients and your team and results in a more involved role for both in the creation and delivery of value.

- You need to communicate your plans to the team prior to defining the client experience but only after defining your vision.

- You must decide if you're willing to change how you communicate with clients and how you recruit and develop your team to ensure that the business reflects your vision.

Your Turn

In this chapter we lay the groundwork for the three key components of the Action step: defining your client experience, your role and your team experience. You'll benefit by co-creating parts of each step with your team, so you may want to communicate your vision to them before starting down that path. To prepare you for the process of communicating your vision to the team, answer these key questions.

Download the full workbook at www.absoluteengagement.com/book and enter the code 'IfNotNow'. The workbook includes room to respond and tips to interpret your answers.

When you sit down with your team, your spouse or a friend, how will you describe the following:
What is your vision for the business?

_____
_____
_____
_____
_____

What needs to change to bring that vision to life?

_____
_____
_____
_____
_____

Why do you feel it's important to make these changes?

_____
_____
_____
_____
_____

ACTION: THIS IS WHERE CONFIDENCE LIVES

How will the team be involved going forward?

_____

_____

_____

_____

_____

Now that you have a good understanding of trends that will influence how you will need to engage your clients and your team, are you willing to change how you communicate with clients and how you recruit and develop your team to ensure that the business reflects your vision?

◯ Yes, I'm continuing down the path to Absolute Engagement

◯ No, my comfort zone is looking good right now

What do you see as the potential barriers at this stage?

_____

_____

_____

_____

_____

What are the specific next steps you will take based on what you have read in this chapter and written about your own business?

1. _____
2. _____
3. _____
4. _____
5. _____

7
ACTION:
THE CLIENT
EXPERIENCE

STARTING POINT:
You have a clear
understanding of the trends
that are impacting client
and team engagement.

THE NEXT STEP:
Design a client
experience that is
tailored to, and aligns
with, your business vision.

An extraordinary client experience is intentional, consistent and meaningful. Its scope includes everything that you deliver to your clients, from the communications you send to the process and structure that you put in place to ensure you're delivering on that experience effectively. And while you may have read or thought a great deal about providing a strong client experience, the key activity that will set you on the path to Absolute Engagement is to design an experience that goes beyond general good service to support the needs, goals and aspirations of your ideal client.

Because the path to Absolute Engagement focuses your attention on creating a meaningful client experience, those who have achieved it believe their clients are more engaged.

But designing a meaningful client experience, when it comes to Absolute Engagement, is about more than providing an engaging experience. Those who are Absolutely Engaged are more likely to believe they are making a meaningful difference.

What does it mean to tailor your client experience? It means that every aspect of what you deliver to clients is driven by the unique needs of your target so that it's highly focused. Assume, for a moment, that your goal is to work with professional football players. When you embrace Absolute Engagement as the goal, you move along this path.

I <u>can work</u> with professional football players

becomes

I <u>do work</u> with professional football players

becomes

I have <u>built my entire business around</u> the unique needs of professional football players

Building your business around the needs of professional football players could mean working directly with their agents, incorporating their family in the process or providing additional education around financial management in face of a potentially brief career. It could mean hiring a team that's passionate about the sport and travelling to meet them where they need to meet. Your process would conform to the target.

. . . .

Evelyn Zohlen is the president of Inspired Financial. Her firm focuses on women in transition, many of whom are working through a divorce or recent widowhood. Evelyn explains that her clients have unique needs at this stage of their lives and as much as working together is about the finances, she hopes to help them look forward to their life after the transition. Part of that entails "lowering the bar" on what can be a stressful facet of their life. She explains that when you walk into their office they have absolutely no technical collateral and do not have CNBC streaming. You won't find the Wall Street Journal sitting in the magazine rack; you'll find Travel + Leisure and Food and Wine and Wine Spectator. When you walk into the conference room, there are maps on the walls and clocks with different time zones hinting at the life ahead for them. Evelyn also says that their vision gets right down to the smallest details like having tissues close at hand and a bowl of chocolates on the table, both of which are helpful when talking about incredibly difficult and often painful issues. "These details may seem small or even silly," Evelyn says, "but they make all the difference in helping a woman relax and feel more confident about the choices she is making with the partner she has selected."

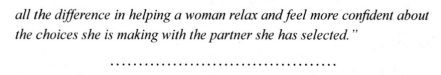

That's how you bring a personal vision to life. Evelyn went from personal passion, to defined business vision to clear process. All aligned.

Creating Your Client Experience

When we examined the first two steps, Awareness and Audacity, we focused squarely on you and your personal vision. By focusing on the client experience, we've added a new element, which is, of course, your clients. As much as I believe that you need to choose the people with whom you work, we also examined the need to co-create the value you deliver. You cannot tell clients what an extraordinary client experience looks like but you can invite them into the conversation to help inform that client experience. To that end, we'll examine client experience by walking through the following four steps:

1. **Involve the client in defining "great."** Actively involve your clients to learn what *they* consider great, based on their experiences with you and elsewhere.

2. **Design an extraordinary and perfectly tailored client journey.** Drawing on input from your clients, define how they will experience working with you, from the moment they become aware of you through initial onboarding through ongoing communication.

3. **Design the structure you need to bring your client journey to life**. Examine and design the elements that need to be in place to deliver on your client journey, including team skills, technology and process.

4. **Measure progress.** Create a defined and consistent process to measure your progress in engaging your clients.

Step 1. Involve the client in defining "great."

In the last chapter we talked about the influence of co-creation in driving value and pointed to the need to actively involve clients. It's time to look at what this means, on a more granular level, for you and your clients.

To involve the client I want to talk about client feedback, but perhaps not in the way you might have thought about it in the past. Traditionally we think of client feedback as a client survey that is designed to measure performance. Instead I'd like to think about client feedback more as a way to gain meaningful insight into what your client experience should look like. Your goal is to go deep and understand how clients define value, what "wows" them and what creates deeper engagement. The Absolutely Engaged do just that.

"I have asked clients for input on what they consider most important to help me structure my offer and experience."

63% Absolutely Engaged

43% All others

Source: AbsoluteEngagement.com

There are several ways to gather this kind of feedback, including written/ online surveys, client advisory boards and client interviews:

Written or online surveys

While this quantitative approach is perfect for measuring performance it's somewhat more limited, but by no means useless, when it comes to gaining insight into the client experience. If you're sending out a survey, you could incorporate questions that gather input on:

- The types of communications or activities clients would value (e.g., articles, webinars)

- The topics clients would like to see covered in those communications/ activities

- How clients would describe their primary financial challenges

Client Advisory Boards

Only eight percent of advisors reported having a client advisory board in a 2015 study conducted by the Financial Planning Association's Research and Practice Institute[16]. I highly recommend them; they're a great way to gather insight on what clients really value. The benefit of the advisory board is that clients have already agreed to participate and have been specifically selected based on your perception of their potential contribution. The potential downside is that your current board may not fully reflect your newly defined target client. Structure your advisory board carefully to ensure that their input reflects the input of your target clients.

Client Interviews

Client interviews can be easily set up with a highly targeted group of clients. You don't need to do much more than invite a client to lunch and ask for his or her time in helping you think about your business. It's rare that one of your clients will refuse and, let's face it, most of us like to be asked for our opinion. Here are two examples of client interview structures that will be incredibly helpful in defining "great."

1. Interviews that help you define great.

In order create a great experience, you'll need a deep understanding of what defines great through the eyes of your ideal client. I'd go even further, and say you need to understand what defines a great experience by looking beyond the confines of our industry.

To take action, consider asking two to three clients if you can add 15 minutes to your review meeting. Ask those clients the following question:

Can you tell me about your greatest client experience?

You might hear the names of firms we often associate with "great," such as Disney, Nordstrom's, Apple or Ritz Carlton. Or you might hear about an extraordinary experience with a local mechanic. The only caveat is that they cannot say that experience is with you. Once you've nailed down the experience, start peeling back the onion to understand why.

You might ask:

- Why did you think of that particular experience?

- How did it make you feel?

- How did you hear about the firm?

- What happened when you contacted them the first time?

- What happened during the process of using the product/service?

- What happened afterward (or on an ongoing basis)?

- What words would you use to describe this firm?

- What were the primary touch points?

By the end of the conversation you'll have a clear understanding of what drives real value and the elements of an experience that clients really remember. Then ask yourself whether or how you can match those elements of the relationship, in your own way.

2. Interviews that assess your value

As much as looking outside the industry is important, that doesn't mean you shouldn't examine how clients perceive the value you provide today. When clients talk about what you provide, they may describe it in completely different terms than you would yourself, or than a prospect might see on your website. Ask the right questions, however, and you'll hear the words that clients use to describe the impact you have had. That's your value.

I recall running a workshop with a group of very successful advisors and asking them to describe a specific client situation and how they would describe the value they provided. One brave soul worked through the exercise with me. He described a very complex estate issue with one of his clients that demanded an extraordinary amount of time and effort on his part, working with the family and the lawyers. I pushed him and asked how he thought his clients would describe the value he provided at the time. He responded that they'd say he provided the expertise they needed to navigate a very difficult situation. I pushed him further and asked him how he thought his clients would describe how they felt and he had this to say. "I think they would say I helped them grieve." Bingo. The client would talk about the emotional impact of the work, not the work itself.

For advisors who've built careers around providing smart, often complex advice, coming to terms with your value through the eyes of your clients can be a difficult task. We often define our role based on technical expertise so that's our default position when it comes to describing our value.

If this is challenging, consider conducting two to three client interviews that focus on your business. Rather than asking about how you can improve, get creative. Ask questions that will uncover how they see the work that you do and the impact you have. You might ask:

- Why did you select me as your financial advisor?

- If someone asked you to describe how we had helped you, what would you say?

- How do you think the work we have done together will impact your financial future? What will be different?

• What was the trigger that made you decide to get financial advice or change advisors? Was there a problem you wanted to solve?

The very act of inviting input from your clients will have a meaningful impact on client engagement. Client feedback is one of the few things you can do in which both the act of executing on the strategy (asking for feedback) and the outcome (making changes in your business) positively impacts client engagement.

In fact, there's a strong relationship between client engagement and being asked for feedback. According to our annual investor research, 83 percent of clients say they have been asked for feedback either formally or informally, dropping to 28 percent when asked if the feedback was gathered formally (e.g., via a survey). Among engaged clients, 44 percent indicated they had been asked, formally, for feedback. Among the others, that dropped to 22 percent.

Beyond the Interview

In the examples above you're inviting clients to describe "great." Interviews are a powerful way to draw important information out of your clients, but even these have some limitations. Whenever you ask clients for their input on what defines "great" you're faced with the limitations of the human brain. Statistically this is reflected in the concept of "stated importance." That is, when you ask clients what is important, they often tell you what they think "should" be important (e.g, investment performance and expertise). It's less that clients are dishonest and more that they simply don't always understand what's driving their own behavior. For example, having a deep personal relationship with you might actually have a stronger statistical influence on engagement. To understand what's driving behavior, you need to focus on "derived importance" (the behaviors that are tied to the outcomes you seek) rather than stated importance. In the words of my mother—do as I say not as a do—because she knew that the 'doing' was more telling.

As we think forward, as an industry, I believe that we'll begin to take what we think of as client feedback to a new level; we'll focus more on client behavior to understand what's most important. For example, you might want to understand what kinds of educational activities would be of most value as part of your client experience. You can look at actual behavior (e.g., if clients are offered two educational events, which did they attend?) or you can look at how they make choices between theoretical options (e.g., if I offered to run a workshop on these two topics, which would you prefer?). The former would provide better information.

Whatever approach you take, the goal is to gather more meaningful information on what clients prefer, with the critical caveat that they need to be faced with the full range of choices. For example, assume you're focused on working with families and one of the ways you support them is to write a blog every week. Some weeks you focus on educating clients about investments and other weeks you focus on helping them think about their retirement. If clients clicked more often on the articles that focused on their retirement, you could rightly draw the conclusion that a great client experience is tied to helping your clients design an amazing retirement. What if, however, you didn't realize that clients would have clicked even more often on articles that related to equipping their children to make better financial decisions—had they been given the choice? You would have drawn a reasonable conclusion based on available information, but you would have missed the most compelling information. That would have been uncovered by asking a different question.

As we continue to professionalize the industry, I anticipate that behavioral data and input will play a role in helping you define your client experience. United Capital is an American wealth management firm that is a leader in this area. They are creating tools that marry engagement, value and data. Their Money Mind® Analyzer helps prospects and clients understand what money really means to them. Their Honest Conversations® exercise, similarly but at a deeper level, helps clients understand their views and plans for money. In both cases, the firm is gathering in-depth information that will help them understand, and respond to, the needs of clients at a deeper, more personal level. This kind of tool is infinitely more effective than simply asking clients about their core challenge or concerns.

In many ways, this example suggests that the discovery process will play an increasingly important role in the way that you understand and respond to your clients. A typical discovery process is, more often than not, designed to understand risk tolerance and family needs in order to create an effective financial or investment plan for a client. Some advisors may go beyond this basic level and ask creative questions about the client's experience of working with other advisors in the past, or what they hope to achieve in the future. But what if that information could be more effectively aggregated? If all of the information you gathered during the discovery process was tracked and analyzed in the aggregate, you'd likely uncover important insights about what is most important to your target clients. You ask clients a lot of questions. Consider how you can track and analyze responses across all clients and you'll be far ahead of the pack.

At a minimum, your goal should be to gather real insight and understanding about what your clients see as important so that you can effectively tailor your client experience.

Step 2. Define an extraordinary and perfectly tailored client experience.

You may have gone through the process of mapping out your client experience by segmenting your clients and then aligning each segment with a service level. Service level might include things like the number of reviews, educational activity or appreciation events. However, I'd like to think about client experience a little differently, using a client journey map. This process puts you in your clients' shoes as you plot out what will be an extraordinary, engaging and perfectly tailored experience.

Creating a client journey map involves identifying key points of interaction and the many ways in which that interaction can take place. As a result, instead of thinking only about "what" you will offer to clients, you are thinking about how they will experience the process. We already know that the Absolutely Engaged are far more likely to map out all aspects of the client experience.

"I have mapped out every detail of the client experience."

Absolutely Engaged — 41%

All others — 17%

Source: AbsoluteEngagement.com

Key to client journey mapping is ensuring that the experience is extraordinary at every stage of the relationship, starting when the client is a prospect. At each step you define what extraordinary looks like and what processes would support you in delivering at that level.

Below is an image that highlights the structure of a possible client journey map. Along the top you'll see the key points of interaction:

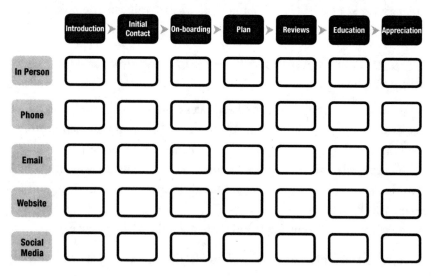

introduction, initial contact, onboarding, plan development, reviews, education and appreciation. You may include different or additional contact points but we'll work with this for our example. Down the side you'll see examples of how a client might interact with you at each stage.

Client journey mapping examines how clients experience each key aspect of the process—how they hear about, connect with and work with you. However, it examines those things based on the many different ways in which people connect with you including phone, email, your website, social media or in person. For example, would a prospect get a consistent message about the work you do if he or she called your office, went to your website, found you on social media or sat in a meeting with you? If you're using this kind of map, you'd note in each box what would constitute extraordinary at each stage and via each form of contact.

The purpose of laying out the journey in this way is that it forces you to think about the client experience at every stage. That's important for two reasons.

First, our investor data suggests that advisors place a great deal of emphasis on delivering on their core activities with excellence, which means that clients are likely to be most satisfied with initial contact and plan development, for example. The data shows lower satisfaction ratings for the other steps (e.g., introduction, reviews, education and appreciation), which suggests that the experience is uneven. It's interesting to note that the areas that receive the lowest satisfaction ratings are those most closely associated with increased referral activity. That means that while we may reassure ourselves that we are putting our energies in the right place by focusing on the core, that uneven experience may cause us to lose out on growth opportunities.

Second, you'll want to look at all of the ways that prospects and clients connect with you because you're looking for alignment. For example, let's assume that being responsive is critical to you and your team. When a client calls your office you've set a standard to pick the phone up within two rings. Or, if a message is left, you are committed to responding to that message within two hours. You may be doing all the right things as it relates to a client call to your office, but what if that client goes to your website? If a client sends a question/comment through the site, do they receive a bounce back note (which seems to have become standard) promising a response within 24–48 hours? Why is that so much slower than the phone? The message is inconsistent, and has the potential to alienate next-generation prospects who don't talk on the phone as much, preferring to email or even text.

Let's look at each stage on the client journey map and ask the big questions to help you tailor and engage at each stage.

Stage 1. Introduction.

The introduction stage begins when a prospect becomes aware of you and your business. It's the first step in the client journey, because your relationship with a client begins before they start working with you. As a result, you'll want the messaging and experience to be consistent and aligned with what a client would experience when they make the choice to work with you.

Achieving the extraordinary, at this stage, is all about clarity around your ideal client, your value and your messaging so that there's consistency in what prospects hear, read and see—on your website, in your marketing collateral, even in the way you describe to prospects what you do in a conversation. That message also needs to accurately reflect what the experience will be like when a prospect becomes a client. Consider the following questions:

• What message do you want to communicate to your ideal prospects to let them know that you are exactly the right advisor for them, whether they were referred or found you some other way?

- If a prospect comes to your website, is your business vision clear or do they see a message that suggests you can work with anyone?

- If a prospect searches for you online, do your social profiles support a consistent message? Can they even find you?

- If they arrived at your office would that same message and positioning be apparent in the office environment, the way they are greeted or the information that is sitting in the waiting room?

- How is the experience, at the introduction stage, specifically differentiated based on your ideal client or offer?

In order to ensure that your message is completely aligned, from your personal and business vision through the experience of both the prospect and the client, you may want to invest time in crafting a clear statement of the value you provide. The way you talk about your value is the link between defining what your ideal business is all about and your ability to express that to your target market. A value statement takes everything that you want to achieve for your ideal client and communicates it in a way that will be meaningful for clients. And it's a key first step with "Introduction."

Think back to the discussion on understanding value through the eyes of your client. You know who you want to work with and you know what you want to offer. The problem is that you may be defining both in your own words, rather than those of your clients. Before moving on to mapping out the rest of your client journey, you should consider how you describe that offer in a way that is compelling for prospects and clients alike. It's important to work on your description at this stage because you'll want that message to be broadcast and reflected across every aspect of your client journey.

Every year I have the opportunity of participating on a number of award committees that evaluate entries from individual financial advisors.

Volunteering this way provides wonderful insight into great businesses from around the world. In one case I was reading the submissions of a group of advisors who were, arguably, some of the most successful in the country. As I read their entries it struck me that I was having a hard time telling them apart. Each one seemed to point to customer service as their prime differentiator, highlighting their "gold standard" and expertise. And that got me wondering. What would value sound like if it were articulated by clients? Would we hear anything about cutting-edge product, gold standard service or leading financial services companies? Probably not!

Here's another, far more personal, scenario (if you'll indulge me for a moment).

Some time ago I went through something that, statistically, many of you will have experienced: I was diagnosed with thyroid cancer. (That isn't the story, but just to fast-forward, everything is absolutely fine.) If we go back 20 years, as I was setting up my first business, I sat with my insurance advisor and she told me some stories about the impact of illness on families in which the person afflicted was the primary breadwinner. That day she insured me fairly substantially. Many years later, I was able to take advantage of that advisor's wise suggestion. So if you ask me about the value that that individual delivered, I wouldn't talk about service or product. I would tell you that she helped me to take some time off and hang out with my (then) two-year-old, and she eliminated the financial concern so my family could focus on getting well and the things that matter most. That's the value she delivered— and I think that stacks up well against someone offering "gold standard service."

So before you go on, you may want to take some time to articulate your value in a simple and concise manner. Just don't use the phrase "elevator pitch." In my view, the elevator pitch is long dead.

The traditional elevator pitch was developed as just that, a pitch. We've all been taught the same thing. When asked what we do for a living, the goal is to respond with just enough information to ensure that the next question is "how do you do that?" or "tell me more." But let's remember that the pitch was structured in this way because we assumed that every breathing individual was a prospect. The goal of the pitch was to lure anyone and everyone into conversation in a way that would have them following you back to your office to sign up. (Think Alec Baldwin in the "Always Be Closing" speech in *Glengarry Glen Ross*).

Now we know that everyone we meet in the proverbial elevator isn't a prospect, particularly as we move along the path to Absolute Engagement. We're not selling the guy in the elevator, we're actually having a real conversation with a real person. What a concept! We don't have to make ourselves sound more interesting. Neurosurgeons don't tell people they help them "reach their individual potential by making full use of their brains." Authenticity matters. The most compelling thing we can say is typically something that reflects what we actually feel is true.

However, the elevator pitch does highlight something very necessary and very important so let's give it a new name and call it a "statement of value." We all need to be able to describe what we do in a way that is clear, meaningful and concise. We can't pull out a PowerPoint presentation at a cocktail party, so whatever we call it—an elevator pitch or something else—it's an important concept.

An effective statement of value balances clarity with understanding and has two parts.

1. **Your role.** This offers clarity. You are a financial advisor or planner, for example, not a psychologist.

2. **What you do.** This creates understanding, by sharing a little more detail on your focus.

Here are a few examples:

- I'm a financial advisor. I work primarily with business owners to grow and transfer their wealth and the value of their business.

- I'm a financial planner. I specialize in helping women feel more secure when they're going through a transition like a divorce or death of a spouse.

- I'm a financial advisor. We take clients through a process to think about the legacy they want to leave and then build a plan from there.

There are a few pitfalls to avoid when thinking about your statement of value.

- **Don't be too cute for your own good.** It's confusing and may negatively impact your credibility.

- **Use words that you would actually say out loud.** Really, say your statement of value out loud and if it doesn't roll off your tongue fluently and naturally, go back to the drawing board.

Stage 2. Initial Contact

Initial contact includes what happens when a prospect reaches out to connect with you directly or online. It includes everything that transpires between making that first contact and actually connecting by phone or in person in a real-time conversation. This step is about setting yourself apart, making a prospect feel welcome and encouraging them to go to the next stage.

Achieving the extraordinary, at this stage, is all about starting to add real value before the prospect even steps into your office, anticipating questions and needs, and communicating that you fully understand those needs because you're focused on working with people like them. This phase is not only about what information you provide but also *how* it is provided, which means using the communication methods that are appropriate for your target audience. Consider the following questions:

- If a prospect connects through your website, do they receive an immediate message that lets them know that you're excited to speak to them, and when and how you'll be in touch—or are they left hanging?

- If a prospect calls your office, does the person who answers the phone share some information on the process, the company and your target market to begin to engage that individual, or just take a name and number?

- If a prospect sets a meeting, do they receive a welcome package with information that reinforces their choice to meet, something that lets them know that you have expertise in working with clients like them as well as basic information like directions to your office? Or, do they simply receive a confirmation on time and date, and a list of documents to bring?

- Do you ask if prospects want to receive the meeting confirmation by email, phone or text? Do you offer web meetings for the prospect or his/her partner if they find it difficult to come into the office?

- How is the experience, at this stage, specifically differentiated based on your ideal client or offer?

Stage 3. Onboarding

Onboarding, quite obviously, refers to the process of bringing a new client into the business. When you think about onboarding you may think primarily about ensuring that you get the technical requirements exactly right, from setting up the account to transferring assets. What you can miss, however, is the fact that this period of time can be variously frustrating and confusing for new clients. As a result, onboarding done extraordinarily well, can create an opportunity to build a deeper relationship.

Extraordinary, at this stage, is all about ensuring clients have a clear picture of the process, demonstrating that they've made a great decision to work with you and anticipating their needs and questions. Consider these questions:

- Do your clients have a clear picture of what needs to happen with the transition and the associated timeline, or will they be left wondering where their money is and how their accounts are progressing?

- Do you give clients the option to bring paperwork to the meeting or submit their information online, based on their preferences?

- Do you anticipate client questions or concerns and ensure that you're proactively reaching out to respond to those questions—even the unspoken ones?

- Do you continue to add value to reassure the client that he or she has made a good decision even during this period of transition?

- How is the experience, at this stage, specifically differentiated based on your ideal client or offer?

. . . .

Jack Thurman wanted to create a Ritz-Carlton experience at his firm. One of the core tenets of the service model espoused by the famous hotel is to anticipate the needs of clients. To that end, Thurman and his team examined all key client interactions to determine if they were effectively anticipating the questions that clients might have, even if not articulated. In particular, they enhanced the onboarding process to proactively reach out when questions were likely to arise. Clients might get to know their advisor but not the leadership of the firm so they receive a personal letter from Thurman after 45 days. They may wonder if all of their funds have transferred successfully. A client service associate calls after 60 days to provide an update. They may have questions when they receive the first statement. Once sent, the advisor calls specifically to review the statement. And a range of other issues and questions could emerge along the way so every new client receives a brief survey asking about the experience after six months.

....

Stage 4. Plan Development

Plan development is the period of time during which you're designing or executing on the plan or strategy you agreed on with your client. This is very much in your wheelhouse but there may be some opportunities to engage that you haven't taken.

Extraordinary, at this stage, is all about connecting the plan to the client's goals and future needs, and focusing clients on the outcome as much as the process. It's about appreciating that clients may want to be more or less actively involved or prefer different methods of meeting. Consider these questions:

- Are you actively engaging couples in the process and ensuring that all questions have been asked and answered?

- Are you involving the client's other professional advisors in the process, as appropriate?

- Are you establishing metrics to track progress that are meaningful to the client? For example, our research shows that older clients tend to focus on investment performance whereas a younger client might want to focus on progress relative to life goals.

- How is the experience at this stage specifically different based on your ideal client or offer?

Stage 5. Ongoing Reviews

This stage refers to one of the most critical touchpoints in the client relationship—your ongoing review meetings. Every bit of research I've conducted with clients points to the importance of this aspect of the relationship in contributing to (or detracting from) engagement.

Unfortunately, it's all too easy to assume that the act of meeting with a client and looking at their plan is enough. We're missing a major engagement opportunity.

Achieving the extraordinary, at this stage, is about actively engaging the client in the process and giving them an opportunity to contribute in a meaningful way by focusing on the issues that matter most (without assuming what they are). Consider the following questions:

- Are you certain that what you are covering in your review meeting reflects what's most important to your clients?

- Are your clients contributing to the meeting agenda?

- Are your reviews inspiring, focusing clients on the future they're building?

- How is the experience, at this stage, specifically different based on your ideal client or offer?

Let's go a little deeper on this one as it's so strongly connected to engagement. Imagine you were in the backseat of the car as your clients were driving home from a review meeting. What do you think you would hear? (Other than "Why is our financial advisor sitting in the back seat of the car?") Would your clients sound energized and inspired? Dazed and confused? Or, would they already have forgotten about the meeting and be discussing what's for dinner that night? Note: The last one is the worst option. So instead of spending too much time worrying about whether you are meeting with clients often enough, you may want to spend more time thinking about what happens when you do meet.

Based on the investor research we've conducted, here's what we know to be true. When clients enjoy their review meetings, good things happen. There's a correlation between the extent to which clients enjoy meeting you and their Net Promoter Score. (Net Promoter Score is a standardized question that asks if a client is likely to refer in the next 12 months.) Fifty-three percent of clients "strongly agree" that they enjoy review meetings; that increases to 75 percent for those who are Promoters (rate a 9 or 10 out of 10 on likelihood to refer).

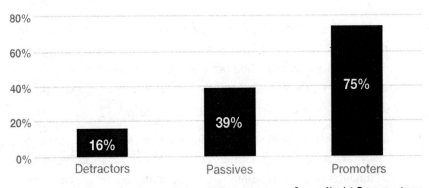

Source: AbsoluteEngagement.com

Q: To what extent do you agree or disagree that you enjoy the process of meeting with your advisor? (Shows percentage who "completely agree.")

By the way, the older the client the more likely he or she is to enjoy the review process. Clients who are 65 years or older are nearly 60 percent more likely to rate the level of enjoyment as a five out of five than those under 50 years of age. Are they naturally more interested at the review or are you simply not making reviews relevant for younger clients? Are they more comfortable and interested because you've helped them understand investing over the years? It's a question worth asking.

Finally, we know that if one spouse is energized and engaged we can't assume the same for both. While 67 percent of clients describe themselves as highly engaged in the review process, only 47 percent of those same individuals describe their spouse/partner as highly engaged. We can proclaim as loudly as we like that we actively engage both sides of the couple, but clients recognize that this doesn't always happen.

There's no doubt that the quality of the client review is as important as the quantity. In fact, when it comes to frequency of contact, clients generally feel their advisor is over-performing rather than falling short. So what can you do to insert some energy into those meetings? Short of singing show tunes and offering a foot massage during the process, you can probably make some changes.

- **Focus on the future.** People are generally more inspired by looking forward than looking back. Yes, you need to spend some time reviewing what has happened but I talk to many advisors who tell me the majority of the meeting is spent looking in the rearview mirror, rather than looking to the future.

- **Change the name of the process.** Some advisors are ditching the term "review meeting" and for good reason. It's about as energizing as watching the proverbial paint dry. What could you call a review that is more inspiring and forward looking?

- **Give clients some (fulfilling) homework.** Ask your clients to plan for something on their bucket list, like a major trip, to discuss at the next review. If they can identify the goal, you can spend time focusing on how and when they can make it happen as part of the plan. I'd rather spend time on an annual "bucket list update" than an annual financial review.

- **Get clients involved.** Actively involve clients in crafting your agenda. There's evidence that a co-created review meeting is considerably more engaging.

Ongoing Communications

Let's shift to the last two stages in the client journey: education and appreciation. I'd put both under the umbrella of ongoing communications although you need to tackle them separately because they meet different objectives.

Extraordinary, at this stage, is all about creating meaningful communications and experiences that will add value and bind you closer to your clients. It's about understanding how they want to experience education and appreciation (in person or online, passive or active), which topics are of interest and where they go for information (professional networks, social media, one-on-one). Some questions to consider:

- Do your communications reflect the unique needs of your target audience or are you trying to provide information that could be of interest to anyone?

- Have you gathered input on what topics or events clients would find most valuable?

- Do your communications inspire your clients to meet their goals?

Stage 6. Education

I hear this all the time: "My clients are working with me because they don't want to get too involved—they want to delegate—and therefore they aren't interested in educational activity." I don't believe it. I travel a lot for work and while I may not be interested in how to fly a plane, I'm interested in how to make travel more efficient and less stressful. It's not that different when it comes to clients.

The reality is that clients *do* value education. When asked to rate the value of the types of communications they receive, clients will almost always place the highest value on what is core to the relationship—client reviews. Next on the list is education, followed by appreciation. There's also a connection between receiving meaningful educational information and client engagement.

There is no shortage of topics to cover when it comes to education. Rather than letting that infinite choice lead in inaction, I'd suggest that you narrow your focus to one or two themes that will resonate with your clients, such as financial literacy for children, Social Security planning or caring for aging parents. Focus on a defined plan that is built around those themes and then leverage those activities across key stakeholder groups: clients, prospects and centers of influence. Squeeze the last ounce of value out of every activity.

For example, let's assume your personal vision is to work with high-net-worth clients who have already made their money and are seeking more meaning in the next phase of their lives. Your business vision is to focus on legacy planning. (I'll use this for my example, but you could just as easily insert multigenerational planning, making your retirement meaningful or tax strategies for business owners—whatever resonates with your clients.)

Here's a sample process:

1. Invest an hour of your time and identify three great articles, from credible sources, that relate to your theme. As you're reading those articles, identify the five most common questions the authors are answering (e.g., how do I define my legacy, how does charitable giving fit into a financial plan, which charities are right for me?)

2. Send an email to clients, highlighting those questions and linking to one of the articles. If you're using social media, link to that article wherever you have a presence. If you have a prospect list, send a copy of that article to prospects. If you work with centers of influence, send a copy of that article with the suggestion that it might be of interest to their clients.

3. Two to four weeks later send the next article, summarizing the key message. Repeat the social media share, prospect and center of influence communications.

4. Two to four weeks later, send the final article with the summary. Include a P.S. that indicates you'll be bringing clients together for a discussion on the topic and they should look for the invite. Repeat the social media share, prospect and center of influence communications.

5. Two weeks later send an invitation to a small event. A legacy planning event might showcase several charities or a speaker who helps clients think about their own legacy. If possible, videotape the presentation.

6. One week after the event, send a summary of the key takeaways from the event and send it to clients, prospects and centers of influence. Create a single slide with those takeaways and post it on social media. If you taped the presentation, select a few key messages and post them on your website. Create a client-friendly summary for centers of influence to share with their own clients.

7. Follow up with key clients, prospects and centers of influence to see if they have questions or want to meet.

The entire client communication campaign takes 7 to 12 weeks to execute. If you did nothing else you would have added significant value for your clients, prospects and centers of influence. The big difference is that you focused your energy on a single theme, which makes you more efficient—and more precise based on the needs of your target client. What's more, you now have a defined process for client education that you can repeat once or twice a year, each time with a new topic that relates to your target. With a repeatable process in place, it's like the shampoo bottle says: Lather, rinse, repeat.

Stage 7. Client Appreciation

Client appreciation has been a part of the thinking advisor's communication mix for as long as I can remember. The goal has always been the same: to let clients know that you appreciate the opportunity to work together. It's hard to argue that telling clients you appreciate them is a bad thing, so I won't try. I will suggest, however, that if you are passively appreciating our clients then you might be missing a significant opportunity to engage.

I believe that client appreciation activities now fall into one of two buckets.

- Passive client appreciation is focused on the act of saying thank you. The objective is to ensure that clients feel appreciated, so you've succeeded when you have communicated that thought. Examples would include cards, social events, inviting clients to charitable events or sending gifts.

- Active client appreciation is focused on helping your clients attain skills or solve problems. The objective is to ensure that you're actively supporting your clients, so you've succeeded when they succeed. Examples include providing clients with access to financial literacy content for their children or running a workshop that looks at stress reduction or how to protect your personal data online.

Put another way, passive appreciation is an acknowledgment of the relationship. The client is involved by "accepting" the appreciation. Active appreciation provides real support. The client is involved by using the appreciation to affect positive change. Neither passive nor active forms of appreciation are bad, but active appreciation transforms this age-old process into a real differentiator. In some respects, effective client appreciation is another form of leadership: It educates, inspires or opens your clients' minds to new possibilities.

Traditional forms of client appreciation typically involve invitations to events that, I might add, can cost a lot of money. The problems are these:

- Clients probably don't want to socialize with you and/or your clients. Nothing personal, but they probably prefer their own friends.

- If you run one major event it will necessarily only appeal to some of your clients. The rest go "unappreciated."

- Anyone can run a good social event. It's nice but it doesn't necessarily bind you closer to your clients.

New forms of client appreciation are less likely to be purely social events and more likely to focus on the things clients care most about. These communications or events will:

- Actively involve the client. Involvement is correlated with engagement (and engagement with referrals).

- Connect you to something important in your client's life, which sets you apart.

- Demonstrate that you know what matters to your clients.

Whatever form your ongoing communications take, they need to reflect the interests and needs of your target market. And we may need to get creative to understand what would be meaningful instead of making assumptions.

- Choices tell you a lot about people so create some. Instead of inviting clients to an upcoming workshop on an issue you consider important, send them a poll in advance and give them a choice of topics. Track and analyze those choices carefully to help you structure meaningful events but also to help you understand what's on the minds of your clients.

- Client behavior speaks volumes about what is most important. Some of the most interesting advances in client communications are technologies that personalize the information clients receive based on their interests. Some systems ask clients about their interests and then curate content on the basis of that input, automatically. Advisor Stream is a good example of this technology. Others are taking it to another level and curating content based on behavior rather than stated preferences. Grapevine6 is an example of this. The system uses social profiles and activity to "understand" what kinds of information would be of interest, and then curates content based on everything from the industry or role of the client to the groups they participate in on LinkedIn.

Hang On, What About Profitability?

We've focused a lot on what "great" looks like, working through each stage of the client journey. You've thought about what would be meaningful and how you would deliver, and you've focused on alignment and value. What we haven't talked about is whether all of this is profitable. It goes without saying that this is an important question.

Everything that we've defined to this point focuses on how you communicate with your clients and what forms of communications would be valuable. In fact, the focus of your communications and messaging have no meaningful impact on profitability either way—but the scope of that communication has a very significant impact. That is to say, enhancing your client reviews to be more engaging and involving the client carries no cost; it's all about approach and process. However, your choice whether to hold one or four reviews with a client annually will profoundly affect your costs and profitability.

For that reason, it's important to note that because we've been talking about the client journey, we can't abdicate responsibility to ensure that what you are delivering is also in line with the value of the client relationship. Let's explore this idea for a bit. Several elements of the client experience that will impact cost (and therefore profitability) include:

- **The number of review meetings.** Will you meet annually or quarterly?

- **The scope of offer.** Will you provide a comprehensive financial plan or a simple projection?

- **The scope of educational activity.** Will you offer quarterly workshops or an annual conference call?

- **The scope of appreciation activity.** Will you send an interesting article or bring in a paid speaker to a client event?

I believe strongly that in order to be profitable in the long run, you need to have a minimum asset or revenue level. The death knell of deeper engagement is overservicing smaller clients in the hopes that they will one day have more assets or needs that will lead to higher fees. In order to tackle this potential profitability problem we tend to tier service levels, which is effective. Tiering, however, has two potential pitfalls:

- By working with clients whose assets are too small to justify the experience you really want to deliver, you're limiting your capacity to add value to other clients. That puts a drain on profitability at a time when you need to reinvest in client and team experience. If you can't invest in a meaningful client experience as a result of tight margins, you'll move off the path that leads to Absolute Engagement.

- You run the risk of stripping down your offer so far that you can no longer attract your ideal client and you no longer feel you're doing meaningful work. At the point that your client experience no longer actively reflects the unique needs of your target audience, you'll move off the path that leads to Absolute Engagement.

While there are pitfalls, tiering service *is* necessary if you have clients who reflect a range of value to the business. You can still tier service while avoiding these pitfalls by ensuring that your smallest clients are still profitable and generate enough revenue to allow you to deliver a meaningful client experience. You may also see tiered service as a temporary solution as you begin to refocus your business on your target client. It won't happen overnight so this allows you to protect your business in the process.

Step 3: Design the structure you need to bring your client journey to life.

With your client journey mapped out, it's time to look inward. Instead of asking what you'll provide to clients, you need to examine how you'll deliver your ideal client experience. To that end, you'll want to consider the following:

- Do you have the right skills to deliver an extraordinary client experience to your ideal clients?

- Do you need to establish new partnerships or alliances to ensure that you can deliver effectively?

- Do your current team members share the same passion for working with your ideal? Do you have the right people?

- How is your process or structure specifically differentiated, based on your ideal client or offer?

The Absolutely Engaged generally feel they have the requisite skills in place to meet their long-term goals. Nearly three quarters of those advisors (74 percent) believe they have the right skills, dropping to 57 percent for all others. Skills are among the list of things you'll need to consider when looking at your target. Other aspects of delivery include:

- Technology

- Process

- Team

- Office

So think about your ideal client, your offer and your client experience and ask what needs to change. Let's use an earlier example and assume you're targeting professional football players as your ideal client. How might your internal processes and structures evolve to reflect the needs of your niche? Would you need to:

- Expand your offer to incorporate basic education/financial literacy for players?

- Extend your educational programs to players' families?

- Create more formal relationships with other professionals (e.g., sports agents)?

- Hire staff based on a passion to help this group of individuals (more on that in Chapter 9 on team experience)?

For now, think about how your internal process or structure will need to change to deliver on the client journey you mapped out earlier.

Step 4: Measure progress.

Finally I'd like to look at how you measure progress in delivering on your client experience. At the outset of this chapter I talked about the role of client feedback in helping you to define (or refine) what extraordinary looks like through the eyes of your clients. We talked about it as a onetime exercise to understand your clients at a deeper level. One of the dangers, of course, is that you'll see client feedback as a "project," something to define and execute, and then move on. However, it's important to design a process to measure your progress in delivering on this experience on an ongoing basis. The client experience is only a success if your clients rate it as a success.

It's at this point that client feedback comes back into the story. Now, however, we're looking at client feedback as a way to measure performance and, importantly, to identify potential changes. Gathering feedback effectively is partly about *how* you gather feedback (e.g., having a formal process rather than relying on informal conversations), but very much about the kind of information you're gathering. Feedback for the sake of feedback isn't helpful. To get a little more specific on the kinds of information you can gather, consider the following as a strong starting point.

- Assess the overall quality of the relationship. You may choose metrics such as satisfaction, loyalty or Net Promoter Score. This information is a starting point for evaluating performance over time and a way to highlight potential problems that require your attention, before they affect your business.

- Assess satisfaction on a range of more specific service issues, such as confidence in the team, frequency of contact or confidence in the plan.

- Assess what is most important to your clients in your relationship. This provides you with insights into what your clients value, and whether that is changing over time.

- Assess client expectations regarding the scope of contact, as well as the form of contact. This information allows you to manage expectations and structure a meaningful service plan.

- Assess preferences with respect to receiving client communications (e.g., newsletters) and the way in which you communicate (e.g., email vs. mail). This information allows you to assess your return on effort with the communications/events that you provide to clients and, potentially, to streamline the communication process.

- Assess specific marketing opportunities among your clients, including referrals, share of wallet and cross-selling opportunities. This information allows you to target your client marketing efforts and increase average revenue per client.

If you' re thinking about conducting a client survey, here are a few things to keep in mind.

- **Ask questions on a range of topics.** The question categories were outlined above. You should ask a baseline set of questions that will form your benchmark but consider adding one or two questions that are more specific or topical at the time you're sending the survey.

- **Keep it short.** An effective survey should take no more than five to 10 minutes to complete, which is about 20 to 25 questions. A shorter survey will increase response rate, but you need to balance response rate against the quality and depth of the information that you gather.

- **Be consistent.** There are no absolutes when it comes to the frequency of surveying. If you're sending a survey, consider doing that every 12 to 18 months and stick to the plan. You may, however, want to send quick polls in between your bigger surveys so that you always have your finger on the pulse of what's on the minds of your clients.

- **Dig deep.** It's not only important to understand how clients rate you on specific aspects of service, but also the value they place on those things. By asking about both, you can prioritize your effort, focusing only on improving those things that are most important to your clients.

- **Ask actionable questions.** It's important to generate feedback on aspects of the business that are within your control. For every question that you want to ask of clients, ask yourself a simple question: How will I change my behavior, or my business, in response to the answers to this question?

- **Set the stage.** Help your clients understand the importance of the survey, not only to your business, but to your ability to meet their needs. A cover letter/email is your best opportunity to build your case and encourage your clients to take an active role in the relationship.

- **Include a deadline for returning the survey.** To analyze your survey results effectively, you'll need to ensure that you receive all responses by a specific date. Two to three weeks is a reasonable time frame, the former if all surveys are online and the latter if you are using paper surveys.

- **Include an incentive to respond.** An incentive to complete the survey should be included and clearly linked to the deadline you have established. A typical incentive includes a drawing for a gift certificate or dinner for two. Many advisors, however, are moving to a charitable donation on behalf of clients as the incentive.

- **Give clients the option of anonymity**. While it's frustrating to get specific suggestions from a client whose name is not included, making the survey name-optional will increase your response rate and encourage clients to respond more honestly. Many researchers will disagree with this comment; I believe it allows you to gather robust data while making it highly actionable.

- **Follow up with all clients.** Send a follow-up communication to your clients, whether or not they responded. It's important for clients who completed the survey to know that you've reviewed their comments and are making changes to reflect the needs they expressed. They need to know it was worth their time to participate.

- **Include an open-ended question.** Include at least one question that asks clients how you can improve the business if compliance permits you to do so. This allows them to compliment or criticize, with fewer restrictions than the other questions.

It's Time to Tell Your Clients

By now, you've brain-stormed, analyzed and dug deep into what really matters. You have a plan, except for one small point: Your clients don't know about it yet. If you've changed your focus in a material way, you may be feeling heart palpitations at the idea of telling clients that they may no longer fit. But you've done the math (that was in Audacity, in case you skimmed over that section) and you know you'll be okay.

To help advisors make the shift to a fee-based business, I conducted research among a group of advisors who had made the transition. There was a projected long-term gain but the perception of short-term pain. As I talked to those advisors and created a blueprint that summarized their input, one thing was clear: Ninety percent of the work that went into making this transition took place before a client was ever told about the process. This allowed the advisors to be confident in the plan, understand the potential pitfalls and objections and get very focused on why they were making the shift. In fact, the first thing most advisors said about doing this successfully is that it had to start with a clear understanding of their "why." Sound familiar?

So it's time to plan out some crucial conversations, the details of which will be entirely dependent on the path you've chosen and the structure of your business today. Remember that if you follow the plan we mapped out, you'll already have had some conversations with key clients about your new positioning. Those conversations should have identified some of the questions that will come your way. Key to an effective transition will be the following:

- Know your 'why' so you can passionately explain why you're focusing your business and the impact that it will have on your clients.

- Be clear on the impact upon each client before you start talking. Is this simply an FYI because they're already part of your ideal, or will the client fall outside the new definition of ideal?

- Know your plan for each client based on what you determined was the best approach. Are you transitioning some clients out? Are you delegating the relationship? Are you doing nothing but want them to be aware of the change in focus?

- If your goal is to continue to work together but the client is not in your target market, let them know the changes they might see and reconfirm your process and the service they can expect. Reassure them. Bear in mind that the primary changes for this group will likely be your website and ongoing communications. Be sure they know that and accept it.

You might consider holding a group webinar or meetings with all clients who fall into your target market. This is all good news for them so you don't necessarily need one-on-one conversations, and a group meeting will save time and money. Treat it like a celebration of those clients, which it is in a way.

So now you have a client experience that will set you apart in the minds of your clients. There are two final and potentially substantial pieces of the Action puzzle and they are you and your team. This plan means next to nothing if you don't have the right people to deliver on it, and if you aren't playing exactly the right role to drive the bus forward. We tackle both in the next two chapters.

The Recap

- An extraordinary client experience is intentional, consistent and meaningful, and must be designed to support the needs, goals and aspirations of the ideal client.

- When you build your client experience around the unique needs of your target, you are creating a direct connection between personal vision, business vision and client experience. That is the essence of Absolute Engagement.

- You cannot tell clients what an extraordinary client experience looks like but you can invite them into the conversation to help inform that client experience by following these steps:

  ○ Involve the client in defining "great," using surveys, advisory boards or interviews.

  ○ Design an extraordinary and perfectly tailored client journey that reflects the key touchpoints in a client relationship: introduction, initial contact, onboarding, plan development, reviews, education and appreciation.

  ○ Design the structure you need to bring your client journey to life, including skills, partnerships and processes.

  ○ Measure your progress to ensure you are on track.

  ○ Ensure that your plan reflects the value of clients to support long-term profitability.

  ○ Communicate your plan to clients with confidence and a clear understanding of the potential impact and objections.

Your Turn

With this step you're beginning to bring your vision to life through the client experience.You'll need to start getting specific about what it means to deliver an engaging client experience that reflects the unique needs of your ideal target client. A client experience that is not influenced by your target audience and offer may create a level of satisfaction, but does not lead to Absolute Engagement.

Download the full workbook at www.absoluteengagement.com/book and enter the code 'IfNotNow'. The workbook includes room to respond and tips to interpret your answers.

What form of client input will you use to understand what your clients consider an extraordinary client experience (e.g., surveys, advisory boards or interviews)?

_____
_____
_____
_____
_____

What methods will you use to understand what is most important to your clients (e.g, describing greatest client experience, providing input on your value or examining behaviors)?

_____
_____
_____
_____
_____

ACTION: THE CLIENT EXPERIENCE

How will you tailor the components of each of the following stages of the client journey to engage and reflect the unique needs of your target audience? Keep in mind that you also want consistency across all touchpoints.

Introduction

_____

_____

_____

_____

_____

Initial contact

_____

_____

_____

_____

_____

On-boarding

_____

_____

_____

_____

_____

Plan Development

_____

_____

_____

_____

_____

On-going Reviews

_____

_____

_____

_____

Education

_____
_____
_____
_____
_____

Appreciation

_____
_____
_____
_____
_____

If you work with a range of clients (in terms of their value to the business), which of the following have you done?

○ Segmented clients based on value

○ Defined the scope of service by segment (e.g., frequency of reviews)

○ Assessed the cost of service delivery by segment

What are your next steps to ensure your plan is profitable?

_____
_____
_____
_____
_____

What aspects of your internal processes or structures will need to change to support the delivery of this tailored client experience?
Personal Skills

_____
_____
_____
_____

ACTION: THE CLIENT EXPERIENCE

Team Skills

_____
_____
_____
_____
_____

Partnerships

_____
_____
_____
_____
_____

Process

_____
_____
_____
_____
_____

Technology

_____
_____
_____
_____
_____

Other

_____
_____
_____
_____
_____

How will you measure progress in meeting the needs of your clients (e.g., client feedback)?

_____

_____

_____

_____

_____

How will you communicate your plan to your clients?
You may want to be prepared to answer these questions.

Why are you focusing your business on a defined target market?

_____

_____

_____

_____

_____

What will the benefit be to me, as a client?

_____

_____

_____

_____

_____

What will happen to me, as a client, if I'm not part of that target group?

_____

_____

_____

_____

_____

ACTION: THE CLIENT EXPERIENCE

What, as a client, can I expect to change in the short term or long term?

_____
_____
_____
_____
_____

What do you see as the potential barriers at this stage?

_____
_____
_____
_____
_____

What are the specific next steps you will take based on what you have read in this chapter and written about your own business?

1. _____
2. _____
3. _____
4. _____
5. _____

8
ACTION:
YOUR ROLE

STARTING POINT:
You've determined what
an extraordinary client
experience looks like.

THE NEXT STEP:
Define the role you will
play and the steps to
make it happen.

Absolute Engagement is not only about your clients and your team but about how you'll spend your time. In the Awareness phase I asked you to think about the work that you (and you alone) should be doing and what you are passionate about. Our data suggests that when you can focus on the right work, the business will experience significant growth. The challenge, of course, is figuring out what to do with everything else (and how you'll pay for it).

Before we examine what drives deep team engagement, we need to tackle the issue of where you will fit in on the team. How you spend your time may influence how you structure your team and who is right for your team.

The plan here is deceptively simple:

1. Define the role you want

2. Figure out how to delegate the rest

When I set up my current business I had to go through this process because I found myself without support. And while it felt terribly entrepreneurial I also knew I needed help. I reached out to a firm called EAHelp to connect me with a virtual assistant. As part of their onboarding process, they also introduced me to their Delegation Matrix Worksheet.

On this simple time-management worksheet, they outline the four quadrants into which virtually all of our activity falls and the actions we should take.

The actions are clear:

- For Q1: Keep doing this stuff.

- For Q2: Delegate this stuff.

- For Q3: Delegate this stuff as well.

- For Q4: Delegate this stuff immediately, if not sooner.

If you translate this matrix to your pursuit of Absolute Engagement, your goal is to focus as much of your time as possible on Q1 activities. I was interested to know how advisors were performing on this and so I did some research, which revealed that only 12 percent of advisors say they spend three quarters of their time (or more) on Q1 activities.

The reality is that most of us can, with relative ease, identify the activities that should be our primary focus—those things that we (and perhaps only we) can do. On the flip side, it won't tax your mental capacity to identify the activities that you definitely shouldn't be doing. Those two extremes aren't the problem. It's the messy middle, the ill-defined set of activities to which we either have an unnatural attachment or simply haven't trained someone else to do.

What I find particularly helpful with this approach is that the four quadrants highlight that messy middle, which forces you to ask yourself some potentially uncomfortable questions. Because the goal is to work toward delegating everything that isn't in Q1, you're forced to come face-to-face with all of those activities you actually like doing but aren't moving you toward your goal. Not delegating them means giving yourself permission to waste time, essentially.

So what do financial advisors put in the quadrants? When I looked at all of the activities they shared, they broke down into six general categories, which will look familiar:

- Client relationships

- Investments/planning

- Growth

- Team

- Strategy/business management

- Administration

There was some general agreement on which activities fell into which quadrants but it was not as pristine as you might imagine. Depending on the advisor, the same activity could land in any one of the four quadrants. However, when we take a high-level view of the data we can begin to see what we might need to do differently in order to focus our time.

1. Defining Q1 activities starts with your core skills. In some cases, there was overlap between Q1 and Q2 activities. For example, some advisors put client meetings in Q1 and others put them in Q2. Still others do the same with team management or investment management. The reality is that there's no right answer to what is in Q1 for you. It's all about defining the role you want to play on the team, based on your unique skills (read, personal vision). For some, building deep client relationships is a unique skill; for others, the unique skill is investment strategy or business vision/growth.

Doing the right activities is also about knowing which tasks will drive the business forward. As a result, focusing on the core may mean giving up something you enjoy (e.g., marketing) or playing a nontraditional role (e.g, not managing client relationships). And that takes us to the next point.

2. Understand what you are giving up. There's a good chance that you'll uncover some conflict between the activities you love and the things that will drive your business forward. If you find yourself tinkering with things that someone else could do, then you're squarely in Q2. The question is, are you willing to give those things up? They likely bring you some element of fulfillment, so it won't be easy. I can't tell you if you should do those activities or not, but it's a choice you'll need to make.

In my view, it's critical to act intentionally and make conscious decisions, even if you plan to continue with a lower-priority activity. If you keep an activity because it brings you joy, then accept the implications for the business and do it—unapologetically.

3. Break big activities down to find delegation opportunities. While some activities in the research appeared to straddle multiple quadrants, upon closer examination we found more nuance. For example, portfolio or investment management appeared in several quadrants—but not so when broken down into its component parts. A more refined breakdown took a big activity, like investment management, and broke it into several more specific tasks. Portfolio strategy might be a Q1 activity, portfolio management a Q2 activity and rebalancing a Q3 activity. Sometimes focusing on the right things means getting more granular about bigger activities. A little analysis will reveal exactly where your role needs to start and stop when it comes to activities like client, team or investment management.

4. Beware the training gap. Much of the overlap between Q2 and Q3 activities can be explained by a lack of training. That is, you continue to do the activities because no one else knows how and you haven't taken the time to teach them. Two distinct challenges emerged in our research.

- A need to invest the time in effective training so you trust others to take over.

- A need to outsource key functions, specifically compliance and IT (and HR for some).

5. The Resource Gap. Where I saw overlap in Q3 and Q4 activities it was often tied to a lack of resources. That is, you continue to do some tasks you shouldn't simply because you don't have enough people. I think the answer is clear: Hire someone. This might be where a freelancer or virtual assistant comes into play, which is why I started this story with EAHelp.

Take Action

The next step shouldn't be surprising—create your own activity matrix. Once that is complete, start asking yourself what might need to change.

- Are the Q1 activities the things I should be doing based on my passion, skills and goals?

- Am I willing to give up some of the Q2 activities to support long-term growth or am I willing to accept lower growth to continue to do these activities?

- Where are the training gaps on the Q3 activities, and what can I do to fill them?

- Do I need more resources to ensure that I'm not doing any of the Q4 activities?

On this path to Absolute Engagement, delegation will be an important part of the process. It will create the capacity you need to focus where you can have the biggest impact. One of the tests of success for many advisors is whether (or for how long) the business could effectively operate without them.

"My business could operate effectively if I had to be away for an extended period of time."

58% Absolutely Engaged

36% All others

Source: AbsoluteEngagement.com

Delegating also buys you the time you need to focus on moving your business to where you want it to go. And now we can start focusing on your team and creating exactly the culture that will support your personal vision.

You might be asking a perfectly reasonable question at this point: This all sounds good, but how do I pay for it? Paying to bring in additional staff is tough, but we know that if you do it to focus your attention on growing the business then there will be a return. If you are hiring staff to take more time off that's a different situation and one you'll need to tackle for yourself. However, the process I've outlined above suggests that every hour of support will lead to an hour of time that you can focus on growth. The return on investment is clear but you might need to cut some costs (including your own compensation) in order to fund the growth.

The Recap

- Absolute Engagement is not only about your clients and your team, but about how you will spend your time.

- When you can focus on the right work, the business will experience significant growth.

- To evaluate your time, put your activities into four quadrants based on the extent to which you are passionate about doing the activity and if someone else can do it.

- Once you have evaluated your activities, ask yourself the critical questions to help you confirm the activities you should be doing, give up activities you shouldn't be doing, identify opportunities to train others on key activities and, sometimes, highlight the need for additional support or resources.

Your Turn

In this step you've started to analyze how you spend your time and, if relevant, laying the groundwork to allow you to focus more of your time on the activities that will drive the business forward.

Download the full workbook at www.absoluteengagement.com/book and enter the code 'IfNotNow'. The workbook includes room to respond and tips to interpret your answers.

What tasks would you put under each of the following headings?

Q1. The activities you love and only you can do.

1. _____
2. _____
3. _____
4. _____
5. _____

What proportion of time do you estimate you spend on these activities?
_____%

Q2. The activities you love but you know that others can do.

1. _____
2. _____
3. _____
4. _____
5. _____

What proportion of your time do you estimate you spend on these activities?
_____%

Q3. The activities you hate but find yourself doing.

1. _____
2. _____
3. _____

4. _____
5. _____

What proportion of your time do you estimate you spend on these activities?
_____%

Q4. The activities you hate and others can do.

1. _____
2. _____
3. _____
4. _____
5. _____

What proportion of your time do you estimate you spend on these activities?
_____%

Looking at each quadrant, answer the following questions.

Are the Q1 activities the ones you should be doing based on your passion, skills and goals? If not, which ones do not fit?

_____
_____
_____
_____
_____

Are you willing to give up some of the Q2 activities to support long-term growth or are you willing to accept lower growth to continue to do these activities?

_____
_____
_____
_____
_____

THE PURSUIT OF ABSOLUTE ENGAGEMENT

Where are the training gaps on the Q3 or Q4 activities and what can you do to fill them?

_____
_____
_____
_____
_____

Do you need more resources to ensure you're not doing Q2, Q3 or Q4 activities?

_____
_____
_____
_____
_____

What do you see as the potential barriers at this stage?

_____
_____
_____
_____
_____

What are the specific next steps you will take based on what you have read in this chapter and written about your own business?

1. _____
2. _____
3. _____
4. _____
5. _____

9
ACTION:
TEAM EXPERIENCE

STARTING POINT:
You've clearly defined
an extraordinary client
experience and the role
you will play.

THE NEXT STEP:
Design a team experience
that supports and aligns with
your client experience and
your business vision.

There are many similarities between creating an extraordinary team experience and creating an extraordinary client experience. There are elements that you need to define, to align with your personal vision, and pieces that you need to co-create with those around you. Get it right and you'll achieve perfect alignment between personal, client and team engagement.

When you began to think about your personal vision for the business you focused on the right clients, right work and right role. As you started to paint a picture in your mind of what you want to create, I suspect you weren't alone in that picture—there was a team around you. Personal vision also extends to your team, your culture and the environment you create. The team experience, however, is also heavily influenced by your client experience because you need the right people in place to take action.

The connection between client and team experience is supported by the research of John H. Fleming and Jim Asplund. They are both chief scientists with Gallup and are, jointly, the authors of *Human Sigma*[17]. In that book they explore the connection between client and team engagement. Based on extensive research they conclude that the team experience and client experience cannot be managed in isolation because creating value is based on the interaction between the employee and the client. They are mutually dependent. This is supported by the notion of true alignment, which of course is the hallmark of Absolute Engagement.

Because the path to Absolute Engagement focuses your attention on creating a meaningful team experience, those who have achieved it believe their teams are more engaged.

"My team is incredibly engaged - a 9 out of 10 or higher."

63%

38%

Absolutely Engaged   All others

Source: AbsoluteEngagement.com

In part, the perception of engagement may be influenced by the perception of impact. The Absolutely Engaged believe they are making a real difference in the lives of their teams.

"I feel that I'm making a significant difference in the lives of my team and give that a 5 out of 5."

82% — Absolutely Engaged

50% — All others

Source: AbsoluteEngagement.com

Team Experience: The Plan

In order to create a team experience that's not only meaningful for the team but supports your client experience and aligns with your personal vision, we'll break the process down into three sections:

Define Your Culture. This is the connection between your personal vision and the vision you have for your team. Vision is defined by you, as the leader.

Get Clear on Fit. This is about defining who is exactly right for your team based on your culture and your client experience. Fit is influenced by your client experience but ultimately defined by you, as the leader.

Create an Engaging Experience. This is about defining a plan that will ensure that your team members are deeply engaged in bringing your vision to life. Engagement includes everything from communication to compensation and appreciation, and is co-created with the team to ensure that it is meaningful.

Step 1. Define Your Culture.

We know that advisors who are Absolutely Engaged take an intentional approach to both designing and nurturing a culture that reflects their personal vision.

"I 'completely agree' that our culture is intentionally designed and nurtured."

78%

50%

Absolutely Engaged   All others

Source: AbsoluteEngagement.com

Culture is unique to you and is inextricably linked to your values, your people and the way you interact. For the great advisors I talk to, they say it's the secret sauce but one that needs to be nurtured. Rebecca Pomering is the chief practice officer at Moss Adams, a Seattle-based certified public accounting and business consulting firm. She had this to say regarding the role of the leader in culture: "Leaders help shape culture and they play a role in sustaining culture. They can also be solely responsible for destroying culture." The day you bring on one team member other than yourself, you have a culture. The question is, what exactly is it?

In the training he provides to his team, Jack Thurman, CEO of BKD Wealth Advisors describes culture as having four components: the set of shared attitudes, values, goals and practices that characterizes an institution or organization (or, I would personally add, a team). Rebecca Pomering boils it down to a simple statement. "Culture is what it feels like to work here." The reality is that culture is everything that happens inside your organization. Sometimes it's easier to recognize it when things go wrong.

Your job, at this point, is to clarify your vision of the culture of your firm or team as part of your personal vision. From there you can look at how your cultural vision is communicated and, critically, how you create buy-in from the team. There are five steps associated with creating and nurturing an effective culture:

1. Assess your current culture.

Start by asking some important questions of yourself. There will be time to bring the team into the conversation. Pullen Consulting Group works with leaders of professional service firms to help them refine their purpose and create alignment among the leadership. According to the firm's president, Courtney Pullen, there are several key questions leaders need to ask of themselves and their firms:

- What is the mood of our firm?

- What do my clients experience and feel when they're in my office?

- How's the communication in the firm?

- Do we avoid difficult discussions?

- How do people relate to each other?

- Do we have a culture of accountability?

- Do we collaborate or tend toward individual silos?

2. Define the culture you want.

To define the culture you really want, Pullen suggests you put the word "Ideally" in front of the answers to each of those questions and rewrite the sentence. Once again, this is all about you and your vision. You'll need clarity to communicate this to the team and to provide leadership.

3. Articulate your purpose statement.

Your purpose statement examines how your culture comes to life in the business. The Table Group is a consulting firm that helps firms enhance what they refer to as their organizational health. The firm's founder (and best-selling author) Patrick Lencioni, suggests you answer these questions and the answers will highlight your purpose:

- Why do we exist?

- How do we behave?

- What do we do?

- How will we succeed?

- What is the most important thing, right now?

4. Refine the process with the team.

Once you have a clear vision for the culture you want to create, invite the team into the discussion. While this is *your* vision, it probably needs to be refined and definitely needs to be meaningful to your team. You'll need them to rally behind the vision in the same way you needed your target clients to rally behind your vision for the client experience.

What does involving the team look like? Just like the client experience, it starts with good information. There are a few ways to consider involving the team and you'll likely need more than just one. This is a nuanced and somewhat complicated process that happens over time. We're not looking for the quick hit.

- Talk to key team members one-on-one to understand what they consider meaningful and have them answer some of those same questions you answered in defining the culture.

- Bring the team together to answer and brainstorm the ideal. Ask them to think about how each element of the culture shows up in the business—from big to small.

- Have an outside firm interview the team to understand how they really feel.

You want to involve the team in helping to refine the culture and that may start with understanding how they perceive the culture. Here's a particularly simple exercise:

Give each person on your team five small pieces of paper and ask each to write down one word, on each page, that describes how it feels to work at the firm or on the team. For simplicity, and to avoid people trying to make things up to fill the time, go with a minimum of three and a maximum of five. Put all the words into the proverbial hat, anonymously, and see what emerges.

- Did team members use positive or negative words? This will tell you something about the mood.

- Did they use words that were the same or, at least, similar? This will tell you if there is focus to the culture.

- Did they use words that you would use? This will tell you if there's alignment.

- Did they use words that reflect what you really want for them? If not, then you have some work to do.

This very simple exercise will work whether you have one team member (except for the anonymity part) or a large staff. Your only job is to analyze the input, without judgment, and define the next step. Your next step will depend very much on the results—but at a minimum it will highlight if and where the culture is out of sync. Because those who are Absolutely Engaged are more likely to actively define and nurture their culture, they anticipate their teams would describe the culture in similar ways.

"I 'completely agree' my team members would all describe the culture in the same way."

46%

26%

Absolutely Engaged　　　All others

Source: AbsoluteEngagement.com

If you're lucky enough to see convergence around a few key themes, then consider another simple exercise. Take the three to five words that reflect the team view of the culture and ask each team member to provide one example of when and how they experienced it in real life. If a team member wrote the word "supportive," for instance, ask for an example of support in action. The reason we do this is tied to the next point, which involves ensuring that your vision is reflected throughout the organization in actions, not just words.

5. Audit the business to ensure everything aligns with your purpose and culture.

Finally—and critically, it's time to audit the business to understand how your culture and purpose come to life. When you examine every part of your business, does it not only reflect, but actively support, the culture you are trying to create? Or—and this can happen easily—are you just paying lip service to a purpose that sounds good on paper or on a plaque on the wall? This exercise is similar to the one in Chapter 7, when you were asked to audit the client experience to ensure that it fully reflected the needs of your target client.

For example, if something goes wrong with a client, how does the team take responsibility? At the Ritz-Carlton they teach that whoever hears about the problem has responsibility for solving the problem.

Here are two quick examples. Not long ago I was on a delayed flight. When I arrived at the airport where I had a connection, I had to change terminals. I asked four different people and each gave me an answer that got me away from them but no closer to where I needed to be. I missed the flight. On that same trip (when I finally arrived), I went to the hotel and asked where I could find the business center. I asked a waiter in the restaurant, who technically had no real connection to the business center. He told me, then said, "You know it's not that obvious," and just walked me a little ways until we could see it. Process can't create that extra level of helpfulness—only culture and a culture of accountability can make service the bones of the people and the business.

Step 2: Get Clear on Fit.

Over many years of talking to successful professionals about their businesses, I've noticed a pattern. In the early stages of their careers, the conversations are all about building the business. Success, however, brings a new set of challenges and new conversations. At that point the conversations turn to the team, often accompanied by deep sighs and wringing of hands.

The good news is that great leaders understand the critical importance of the team to the success of the business. With that in mind, they get to work and focus on structure, development and compensation. Despite that focus, there seems to be one issue that defeats us: finding the right people. The people you hire will make or break your culture. Knowing who isn't right is as important as knowing who is.

Based on the comments I hear, it would be easy to believe that skills and intelligence are in short supply among the general population. We know, of course, that isn't the case. Finding good people isn't actually that hard. Finding the right people for your business, however, is a very different challenge.

It should go without saying that the right team member has the right technical skills. It shouldn't stretch our imaginations too far to create a baseline list of technical skills required to do a specific job well. The right team member also needs the right soft skills. This blinding flash of the obvious suggests that if a team member will be on the frontline with clients, they should be friendly, caring and communicative. However, with Absolute Engagement, we're talking about finding the right people to actively support your vision and target client.

A great team member not only does his or her job well, but is a reflection of your brand. As a result, the team needs to have the same passion and commitment about working with your clients as you do. This is particularly important if you're working with a defined target client or in a niche market. If you work with business owners and your team isn't energized by business owners, you have a problem.

The greatest businesses don't just hire for skills, they hire for fit—fit with your existing team, your culture and your clients.

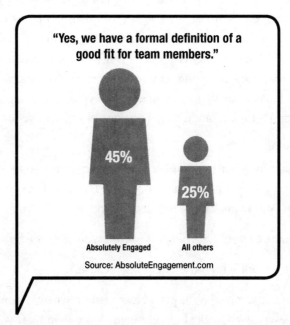

At Brighton Jones in Seattle, the concept of fit isn't just an idea, but it has, quite literally, become part of the environment. They hired an outside firm to interview their key stakeholders as part of an overall branding initiative. One of the outcomes of that process was to get very clear on the words that clients and team members use to describe their team. A "word wall" features prominently at the company's office and highlights the words that matter to the company and its culture, like genuine, approachable, focused and driven. That wall serves as a reminder of who is a good fit for the firm and helps support shared values. According to Jon Jones, Co-CEO, "If any one person is not living the mission, vision and values, you have to wonder why they're here. If you tolerate something outside the core values, you stand for it."

Ask the Tough Questions

Ensuring that fit is right starts with your existing team. They need to be right based on their skill sets, of course. And their strengths must match your needs. (There are a number of tools you can use to assess these areas, including Kolbe and Strengths Finder.) But there is a potentially bigger question to ask. Does everyone on your team share your passion for your ideal client? Earlier I challenged you to define your target market in a way that was meaningful and authentic. This is a great exercise for your team as well.

Ask each team member to complete the same exercise you did earlier to ensure that they fully understand the vision. Hint: It needs to be equally authentic for your team. The two questions are:

At <insert name of your firm here> we work with clients who... .

The reason we work with those clients is because... .

With this quick exercise you'll get a clear read on whether your team can accurately describe your ideal target client. More than that, you'll assess whether they share your passion for working with that group of people. If the team doesn't share your personal vision, you won't succeed in building a business that attracts that target client.

Of course this raises the thorny issue of what you do with people who don't fit the bill. They may not be bad employees, just a bad fit. If this is the case, you may need to help them find a new position. The results of the exercise above are a good place to start. The reality is that if the employee is not a good fit, based on the culture or vision of the firm, they aren't likely happy either. This exercise will make that clear for both of you. If that's the case, have a heart to heart about what that means, reiterate the future focus of the firm and determine if this can be a good fit in the long run. If they don't ever see themselves aligning with the vision, then you may need to do what you can to help them find a new position.

Step 3: Create an Engaging Experience.

The team experience is about the more tactical elements of working with and engaging your team. While the touchpoints differ from client experience, the goal is very much the same—to create an experience that reflects their unique needs, to actively involve them in the process and to drive deeper engagement.

Gallup is one of the leading experts on team engagement and the creator of one of the most commonly used tools to measure engagement (Gallup Q^{12} survey), as well as one of the most popular methodologies for assessing team strengths (The Strengths Finder). The team at Gallup provides a simple but highly effective categorization of team members:

- Engaged employees work with passion and feel a profound connection to their company. They drive innovation and move the organization forward.

- Not engaged employees are essentially "checked out." They're sleepwalking through their workday, putting time—but not energy or passion—into their work.

- Actively disengaged employees aren't just unhappy at work; they're busy acting out their unhappiness. Every day, these workers undermine what their engaged coworkers accomplish.

Dan Pink is the author of five books, including *Drive: The Surprising Truth About What Motivates Us*. In that book he adds some clarity around the drivers of engagement when he refers to three key drivers:

- Mastery, which focuses on helping team members enhance and stretch their capabilities.

- Autonomy, which focuses on providing team members with some autonomy over various aspects of their work.

- Purpose, which focuses on helping to connect team members to a cause that is bigger than themselves.

When you think about the team experience (which we'll do next) are you working toward incorporating these three things? And while the details of every aspect of managing a team are beyond the scope of this book, you may want to assess how you are doing in each of the following seven areas.

1. Understand. Just as with clients, an effective team experience is built around the unique needs, interests and preferences of your team members. To that end, you'll need to get inside their heads and understand more about what energizes and inspires them.

- What are their long-term goals?

- What challenges and energizes them?

- What do they love/hate to do?

We know that the Absolutely Engaged are more likely to formalize the process if inviting input.

"Yes, I have asked the team for input on what they consider most important to understand how I can best support them."

79% Absolutely Engaged

59% All others

Source: AbsoluteEngagement.com

2. Develop. Development focuses on how you support the team in growing both personally and professionally. To do that you' ll need to ask yourself (and your team members) some key questions:

- What skills do they need to develop?

- What skills do they want to develop?

- How do they see themselves contributing to the long-term vision of the business?

Among the specific things that great firms are doing in this area are formalized mentoring programs (internal mentors or support in finding a mentor), in-house universities and setting defined budgets to provide financial support for team members who want to take external courses.

Those who are Absolutely Engaged are twice as likely to have a formal plan in place for staff development, in contrast to a more informal or ad hoc plan.

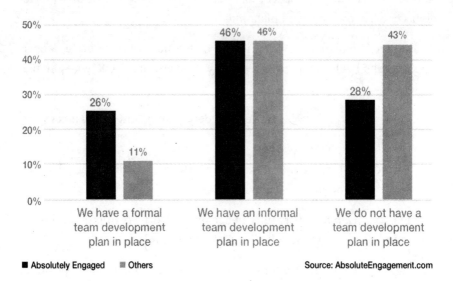

Absolutely Engaged ■ Others   Source: AbsoluteEngagement.com

Q: Which of the following best describes the way you develop your team?

3. Communicate. Communication is about the process and structure you put in place to communicate with the team about day-to-day activities as well as about the future of the business. Ask yourself the following:

• Do you have a way for the team to communicate about day-to-day activities and client issues?

• Do you have a process in place to bring the team together to plan for the future of the business?

• Do you give the team an opportunity to drive parts of the communication process so they have greater ownership?

Among the things that great firms are doing to support meaningful communication is separating meetings to support different objectives: daily huddles to discuss clients or other immediate issues; monthly meetings to discuss broader issues or projects that don't relate to the day-to-day issues that emerge; quarterly planning sessions that assess progress against goals and identify tactics, if needed, to close the gaps; and annual off-sites to focus entirely on long-term planning.

4. Involve. Involving the team is one of the best ways to drive deeper engagement by formalizing a two-way conversation. Ask yourself the following:

• Do you actively involve the team in determining how you'll meet your goals?

• Do you give team members an opportunity to "drive the bus" by sharing information in team meetings?

• Do your team members fully understand the drivers of profitability in your business and the role they play in the firm's success?

Among the things that great firms are doing is rotating the "chair" position of team meetings to give everyone a chance to lead, asking team members to share key findings from a report or conference they attended or creating an expectation that everyone will contribute actively to team discussions.

5. Recognize. Recognition includes both your compensation structure and other rewards you may offer to let the team know they've done a great job. Ask yourself the following:

- Does your compensation structure encourage your team to reach the goals and vision you've set?

- Do you have a way to acknowledge team members who've gone above and beyond?

- Do you have a way to acknowledge team members who are bringing culture, vision or values to life?

Among the things that great firms are doing is creating a process for peer-recognition and reward, providing non-monetary rewards when someone does great work or formally recognizing the efforts of team members and their specific contributions at team meetings.

6. Measure. Measurement is about having a plan in place to ensure that you're delivering on the engagement goals you have set for the team. Ask yourself (and your team members) the following:

- Are team members fully engaged?

- Do they feel they are rewarded and acknowledged in a meaningful way?

- Do they feel they're able to contribute to the long-term vision of the firm?

Among the things that great firms are doing is structuring formal interviews or surveys to gain a better understanding of what matters most to the team, what defines a meaningful reward, how they perceive their roles and what they want to accomplish. Those advisors who are Absolutely Engaged are also more likely to set defined goals regarding team satisfaction (46 percent) compared with all others (24 percent) and more likely to gather formal feedback.

"Yes, I have asked the team for their input on what they consider most important, so that I can understand how to support them effectively."

79%

Absolutely Engaged

59%

All others

Source: AbsoluteEngagement.com

7. Have fun. We shouldn't forget to leave room for having fun as a team. A meaningful process here depends on what's important to your team and the culture you've created. Don't assume. Ask yourself the following:

- Does the team come together to do activities that reflect shared values?

- Do team members enjoy spending time with one another?

- Do you consciously recognize that everyone needs time away to recharge?

Among the things that great firms are doing are firm-wide charitable activities and creating team-led social committees.

Combining Client and Team Experience

Great firms also get creative on combining client and team experience. Two examples follow of how teams are saying "thanks" to the team while learning more about what constitutes a great client experience.

....

Zappos sells shoes but is renowned for its customer service. Tony Hsieh, the company's founder, has become one of the leading voices in what it means to deliver an outstanding client experience. Barry Glassman, CEO of Glassman Wealth, shared a story of how he used Zappos to help his team align around a clear definition of extraordinary service. Barry asked each of his employees to order two pairs of shoes via Zappos. This is my kind of research; it involved shoes and cost less than $1,000. He then asked each team member to return one pair of shoes, leaving the first as a gift. At that point the team got together and shared their experiences, of both the purchase and of having to make a return. I imagine they discussed the process, the interface, the connection with customer service. More important, they would have discussed how they felt at each stage, what made an impact and what made this experience different from other experiences.

....

Ritz-Carlton is one of the most recognizable names when it comes to the client experience. In fact, they are so closely connected with great service that they have developed training programs that teach people across industries how to deliver a Ritz-Carlton standard of service. Fritz Brauner is the president of The Brauner Company and he has also helped his team truly experience what a great client experience really feels like. Here's what he shared with me recently: "Once a year we take our team on a field trip to the Palo Alto Four Seasons for lunch. The purpose is for them to see what exceptional service feels and looks like. Back at the office we ask each team member what they noticed, what stood out, and how we might do the same with our clients. Even something as simple as greeting people with 'Welcome to the Four Seasons' has been incorporated by greeting clients when they come into our office with 'Welcome to The Brauner Company.'" A small thing but everything counts.

....

THE PURSUIT OF ABSOLUTE ENGAGEMENT

The obvious benefit of this approach is the active involvement of the team. By engaging in this kind of collaborative learning activity, you create a shared experience and, in the process, you create buy-in, pride, ownership and commitment.

Which Comes First–Structure or People?

In his management classic, *Good to Great*, Jim Collins argues that you need to "get the right people on the bus" as a precursor to executing your strategy. In essence, you build the business around the right people. In this case I would respectfully disagree. "People first" may be an effective philosophy at an executive/corporate level. However, for financial advisors, I think that structure and culture come first. That means we start by defining the structure and skills that fit with the culture we want to create and the requirements of delivering on the client experience. Then we hire to ensure fit.

I'd go further to say that one of the biggest mistakes we can make—and one of the things that can derail you on the path to Absolute Engagement— is assuming your team is fixed, and trying to build the business around the skills and attitudes that you have on the team today. If you try and bend the client experience to fit with your existing team you may be setting yourself up for failure. It's my sincere hope that the team you have in place is exactly the right team and that they'll embrace this path you're on with much the same energy you have. If that isn't the case, however, you have some tough choices.

I'm an advocate of building an organizational chart with no names as a starting point on structure; you may want to try this exercise. Think about the roles that will be required to deliver on the client experience you mapped out in a previous chapter. Create all of the roles (and reporting lines), even if there are more boxes than people on your team.

Then, think honestly about who would be the best person in each box, irrespective of role. You may find some team members don't seem to fit. You may find that in certain areas, you don't need to manage the process, but would be better off "reporting to" one of your team members. For example, if someone on your team has overall responsibility for marketing but you create great content, then you don't need to take responsibility for marketing; you need to support it with great content.

Taking a Team Approach

A final note on team structure. When you think about "who's on the bus" in the language of Jim Collins, it's easy to think purely about who can line up behind you to support you in delivering on the client experience you've defined. There is, however, an important distinction between having a team and taking a team approach to managing your clients. When you have a team, you have support and you are, very likely, the face of the business. Clients call you for everything and you delegate as needed. In this scenario *you* represent the long-term value of the business. A team approach is different. In this scenario you hire in order to deliver different expertise and the team works directly with clients when appropriate. The team is the business and value is increased because it does not sit with one person. It probably goes without saying that I'm an advocate of the team approach.

The Decision

As you complete step three, which includes action on client experience, role and team experience, you'll come to the next crossroads. Your decision is this:

Will you redefine the client and team experience so that they fully reflect the needs of your target market? Or will you continue to focus on delivering "great service" which is not targeted to your ideal client?

In the next chapter we'll look at how to begin to focus more intentionally on the "life" side of the business equation, starting with creating personal accountability.

The Recap

- An effective team experience needs to align with your personal vision and is co-created with those around you.

- The team experience and client experience cannot be managed in isolation because creating value is based on the interaction between the employee and the client.

- To map out an engaged client experience follow these three steps:

  - ° Define your culture to connect your personal vision with the vision you have for your team.

  - ° Get clear on fit by defining who is exactly right for your team based on your culture and your client experience.

  - ° Co-create an engaging team experience, including development, involvement, communication, reward and fun.

- Those who are Absolutely Engaged:

  - ° Intentionally design and nurture their team culture.

  - ° Engage team members with a focus on mastery, autonomy and purpose.

  - ° Invite team input when designing the team experience.

  - ° Recognize team members based on how well they reflect the values of the firm.

  - ° Measure team engagement on an ongoing basis.

  - ° Structure the work required to deliver on the client experience and then assign to the team rather than building the process around existing skills.

Your Turn

In this step you focused on designing a team experience that supports, and aligns with, both your client experience and your business vision. Remember that the way you structure your team is not only about your ability to deliver on the client experience you have mapped out, but about the kind of environment that you want to create.

Download the full workbook at www.absoluteengagement.com/book and enter the code 'IfNotNow'. The workbook includes room to respond and tips to interpret your answers.

Define Your Culture

How would you describe your culture today?

_____

_____

_____

_____

_____

The following questions will help you assess your current culture

What is the mood of your firm?

_____

_____

_____

_____

What do your clients experience and feel when they're in your office?

_____

_____

_____

_____

_____

ACTION: TEAM EXPERIENCE

How is the communication in the firm?

_____

_____

_____

_____

_____

Do you avoid difficult discussions?

_____

_____

_____

_____

_____

How do people relate to each other?

_____

_____

_____

_____

_____

Are people dropping the ball (underperforming relative to expectations)?

_____

_____

_____

_____

_____

How would you describe the culture you want to create?
Ideally, what is the mood of your firm?

_____

_____

_____

_____

_____

THE PURSUIT OF ABSOLUTE ENGAGEMENT

Ideally, what do your clients experience and feel when they're in your office?

_____
_____
_____
_____
_____

Ideally, how is the communication in the firm?

_____
_____
_____
_____
_____

Ideally, how do you handle difficult discussions?

_____
_____
_____
_____
_____

Ideally, how do people relate to each other?

_____
_____
_____
_____
_____

Ideally, how is the team performing relative to expectations?

_____
_____
_____
_____
_____

ACTION: TEAM EXPERIENCE

How would you describe the purpose of your firm? Why do you exist?

_____

_____

_____

_____

_____

How will you get input from the team as to how they define the culture today and the culture they would like to create?

_____

_____

_____

_____

_____

What are specific examples of your culture in action?

_____

_____

_____

_____

Get Clear on Fit

What characteristics does a team member need to have to be a good fit?

_____

_____

_____

_____

_____

How will your client experience influence what makes a good fit?

_____

_____

_____

_____

THE PURSUIT OF ABSOLUTE ENGAGEMENT

Do you have team members who are not a good fit? What will you do about it?

_____

_____

_____

_____

_____

How will you assess if team members are passionate about executing on your personal and business vision?

_____

_____

_____

_____

_____

Create an Engaging Team Experience

How will you tailor the components of each of the following stages of the team experience to ensure it reflects your vision and is engaging for the team?

Understanding what is important to the team

_____

_____

_____

_____

_____

Creating a meaningful team communications plan

_____

_____

_____

_____

_____

ACTION: TEAM EXPERIENCE

Actively involving the team in the business

_____

_____

_____

_____

_____

Recognizing team members for their individual contributions

_____

_____

_____

_____

_____

Measuring team engagement

_____

_____

_____

_____

_____

Ensuring the team has fun at work

_____

_____

_____

_____

_____

Now that you've translated and identified the components of your ideal client, work and role, will you re-define each so that they fully reflect your personal and business vision?

○ Yes, I'm continuing down the path to Absolute Engagement

○ No, my comfort zone is looking good right now

What do you see as the potential barriers at this stage?

_____

_____

_____

_____

_____

What are the specific next steps you will take based on what you have read in this chapter and written about your own business?

1. _____

2. _____

3. _____

4. _____

5. _____

PART FOUR: YOU'RE HUMAN. DON'T FORGET IT.

Sustaining a great business demands accountability and renewal in equal doses. Absolute Engagement sits at the intersection of business and life; it is as much about building a business that supports the life you want to live as it is about ensuring that your life feeds your capacity to do the hard work associated with intentionally designing a successful business. This principle reminds us that to take effective action we not only need support, we also need to be intentional in how we refresh and renew.

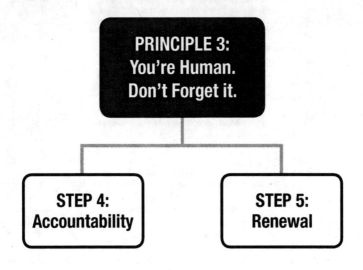

PRINCIPLE 3:
You're Human.
Don't Forget it.

STEP 4:
Accountability

STEP 5:
Renewal

YOUR PATH TO ABSOLUTE ENGAGEMENT

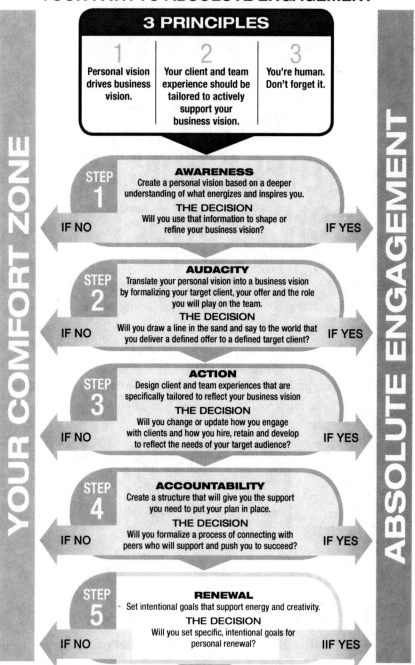

3 PRINCIPLES

1 Personal vision drives business vision.

2 Your client and team experience should be tailored to actively support your business vision.

3 You're human. Don't forget it.

YOUR COMFORT ZONE

ABSOLUTE ENGAGEMENT

STEP 1 — AWARENESS
Create a personal vision based on a deeper understanding of what energizes and inspires you.

THE DECISION
Will you use that information to shape or refine your business vision?

IF NO | IF YES

STEP 2 — AUDACITY
Translate your personal vision into a business vision by formalizing your target client, your offer and the role you will play on the team.

THE DECISION
Will you draw a line in the sand and say to the world that you deliver a defined offer to a defined target client?

IF NO | IF YES

STEP 3 — ACTION
Design client and team experiences that are specifically tailored to reflect your business vision

THE DECISION
Will you change or update how you engage with clients and how you hire, retain and develop to reflect the needs of your target audience?

IF NO | IF YES

STEP 4 — ACCOUNTABILITY
Create a structure that will give you the support you need to put your plan in place.

THE DECISION
Will you formalize a process of connecting with peers who will support and push you to succeed?

IF NO | IF YES

STEP 5 — RENEWAL
Set intentional goals that support energy and creativity.

THE DECISION
Will you set specific, intentional goals for personal renewal?

IF NO | IIF YES

Complete the steps and you'll be at the intersection of financial success and personal fulfillment. The Absolutely Engaged report higher revenue, less stress, better health and more time spent doing the work they love.

10
ACCOUNTABILITY: THIS IS WHERE COMMITMENT LIVES

STARTING POINT:
You've defined a personal vision, translated that to a business vision and mapped out a plan to ensure that your client and team experience are fully aligned with that vision.

THE NEXT STEP:
Create a structure that will give you the support you need to put your plan in place.

Absolute Engagement is about intentionally designing a business that supports the life you really want to live. It's equally about designing a life that supports your capacity to do just that. We turn now to the "life" side of the equation and the first step in helping you achieve the goals you've set.

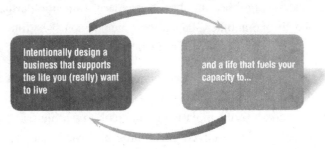

Intentionally design a business that supports the life you (really) want to live

and a life that fuels your capacity to...

Accountability is about ensuring that you have the personal support you need to follow through on your goals. This is where commitment lives, because it forces you to put a process in place to help you take action and stay focused. Those who are Absolutely Engaged adopt formal and informal structures to hold themselves accountable and to help them take action; they build an extended network of people who have their backs. And that means they've started with an understanding that they can't necessarily go it alone. In this step you'll create a structure to provide you with motivation and support to stay the course on the path to Absolute Engagement.

Being an entrepreneur is a lonely business. And while most wouldn't have it any other way, it demands extraordinary focus and self-motivation. On the path to Absolute Engagement you'll be making significant decisions about your business and your future and none of those will come easy. You'll find it helpful to make sure that you have your own support network in place to help you think through your plans and to provide you with the motivation that everyone needs to keep going. In a corporate environment you may have a leadership team with whom to share the burden. As an entrepreneur you'll need to create your own support network.

Where do You Turn for Support?

There's an interesting phenomenon called the Michelangelo Effect[18]. The name comes from research that shows that interdependent individuals influence and "sculpt" one another, particularly romantic partners. How you respond to one another shapes the other person over time and that impact might be positive, neutral or negative.

In action, the Michelangelo Effect sounds something like this: You get all fired up about a big opportunity at work, perhaps similar to the kind of change you might be contemplating on the path to Absolute Engagement. You're excited, you're resolved and a little bit proud that you've made the decision. You get home and you can't wait to tell your spouse about it. The next few minutes are tightly tied to your success because a lot is riding on how that other person reacts. If you get something akin to "Well [sigh], that sounds like you'll be working late then, I guess I'll deal with the kids," it limits your chances of success, no matter how determined you may feel. Perhaps more important, that initial reaction can stop you from taking action at a subconscious level.

But the Michelangelo Effect works the other way as well—your partner's enthusiasm will feed your own passion and make your success more likely. That's important if you're going to start soul-searching and making profound changes. You need a person or a group of people who have your back, who'll tell you the truth and who feel invested in your success. Absent this kind of community, things are going to get very difficult.

So where are you going to find support? Family and friends are the likely first source—but what if you need something more and what if family and friends simply aren't the best people to support you?

. . . .

On Sept. 27, 2015, I managed to walk 70,000 steps for cancer research. That was 26.2 miles following the Boston Marathon course and it was, at least for me....really hard. I don't mean "I'm having a tough day" kind of hard; I mean "I've fallen and I can't get up" kind of hard. What I learned had less to do with the walk itself; the big lesson was in the lead up to the walk. One of the best things I did was join a Marathon Mastermind Group—a small group of walkers, all with similar goals. We met weekly via an online meeting tool and did a couple of important things. First, we used the time to tap into the power of the group to research best practices. One week someone was given responsibility to research what we should eat and drink on walk day and another week someone else did research on the best shoes to wear. As a result no one person was completely responsible for all the research and everyone could tap into more ideas. Second, we used the process to support one another. Each person had the opportunity to share a challenge. It might be lack of motivation around training or fear about not finishing. With the problem out there, everyone focused on trying to solve that problem, drawing on their own experience. This kind of focus meant that if you were the person tabling the challenge you walked away with tangible ideas and insights. In the process of participating in the Mastermind, we tapped into a resource that held us accountable and made us all better.

....

And that process started with a question. *What if the people around you refused to let you fail?*

The Mastermind Group

A Mastermind Group is a group of people who meet on a regular basis to share their experiences and ideas, and create accountability to support mutual growth and development—like my marathon group, but in business. Meetings are held in person or virtually and typically each participant is given time to check in and share a specific issue or challenge with the group. At that point all eyes and ears are on that person. The power of the group is focused on each individual at some point during the call and therein lies the power.

The concept of a Mastermind Group isn't new; Napoleon Hill is often cited as the source of the idea when he wrote *Think and Grow Rich* in 1937. Some of the most successful advisors I talk to have created a structure like this to support their success. It might be a study group or a Mastermind group. And while the two can look quite similar, Mastermind Groups follow a certain set of rules.

Broadly speaking there are two types of Mastermind groups:

The first type is issue- or goal-specific. Like the group I described, a group comes together to discuss a specific topic or objective. For us it was: "How are we going to survive walking 26.2 miles?" For you the objective might be:

• Building an effective online presence

• Working effectively with families

- Building an engaged team

- Increasing referrals

- Targeting younger clients

The second type of Mastermind Group is ongoing, and members discuss goals and challenges as they arise. Many (if not most) groups are ongoing and are more broadly focused on helping individual members overcome specific challenges. It would be incredibly powerful to create a Mastermind Group that included individuals who were all on the path to Absolute Engagement.

Whatever structure you choose, the big difference between a Mastermind Group and a study group is that the entire group is 100% focused on helping each member solve individual problems that they have raised and defined for the group. That kind of brain power, focused on your problem or challenge, is incredibly powerful.

5 Steps to Forming a Mastermind Group

1. Define Your Purpose

Know exactly what the group is trying to accomplish. Everyone in the group needs to be completely supportive of that singular purpose.

2. Create Some Guidelines

As with any group endeavor, it's much easier to determine the guidelines up front rather than when a problem arises. Consider the following:

- How will you make decisions?

- Who facilitates the session?

- What are the rules of engagement (e.g., no whining)?

- Who can be part of the group and when is someone no longer right for the group?

- How confidential is the information you discuss and share?

- Are there consequences if someone misses multiple meetings or is often late?

3. Assemble Your Team

You might be lucky enough to find an existing group. If not, then starting your own may be the best idea. If you're starting the group, think long and hard about the kind of people you want to invite. You want to learn from them and, at the same time, feel confident you have something meaningful to contribute.

Liking the people in your group is a necessary but not sufficient condition of membership. This is about bringing the right expertise and experience level together. Most Mastermind Groups are self-formed and regulated. However, there are an increasing number of groups being launched and managed by industry experts.

4. Determine How You'll Meet

Some Mastermind Groups are held in person and many are virtual. There are inexpensive ways to hold video meetings with as many as 25 heads on the screen at one time. And while 25 is really too many people, using video technology will have a significantly positive impact on your chances of making even a small group successful. You need to see people's faces to make a deeper connection and, of course, the presence of the video camera keeps people focused on the meeting instead of checking emails.

Also think about frequency here. Some Masterminds are monthly, others quarterly and a few bring people together for an in-depth planning session each year. You can mix and match the approach depending on how much time and money you want to invest in the process.

5. Set the Agenda

This is a really critical part of the Mastermind process. The basics are these:

- If someone has an issue they want the group to address, they submit it in advance or at the outset of the meeting. In one of my groups we try to provide sufficient context before the meeting so that the others have time to consider the issue.

- During the meeting each person who raised an issue takes a couple of minutes to present the issue, background and objective.

- Each person in the group has time to ask questions (without providing solutions).

- Once all questions have been answered, each person offers up some solutions.

- The person who raised the issue recaps what he or she heard and what steps he or she plans to take—and then checks in at the start of the next meeting to confirm that those things actually happened.

To sum up, there are three things about the Mastermind process that drive enhanced performance.

- **Content.** Access to great ideas from peers.

- **Community.** A forum for you to gather immediate input and insights into specific challenges from those in a similar position.

- **Accountability**. A process to help you follow-through by building in clear next steps and accountability.

There's another benefit to working closely with others who have the same (or higher) level of success and ambition as you. They inspire you to do more. In many ways, this impact mirrors the plus/minus rating used in hockey and basketball. The plus/minus rating (through the lens of my limited sports knowledge) rates the impact of a specific player being on the field or court. The higher the rating, the greater the impact. You can witness a similar effect in business—and perhaps in life. When you surround yourself with people who are outstanding in what they do, they raise your game as well. When you bring your group together, remember to invite people who will have a net positive impact on the performance of the entire team. Surround yourself with those who inspire you to do more.

What If I'm a Loner?

If you're someone who would be far happier never being in a group situation, then the concept of the Mastermind Group may not be ideal. Ultimately you just need to find *someone* who understands what you are trying to do and who can provide some support. That might be a spouse or a colleague. The key is to be structured in your approach (e.g., a monthly lunch meeting)—otherwise you won't get the support you need.

You may also want to schedule a meeting with yourself at a defined time each week or month to review your goals and ensure you are on track. You can use the workbook that I've created to support your pursuit (which you can access via the URL that appears in each of the exercise sections). In the workbook, I've asked you to work through the key exercises and then define your next steps and create a timeline. You can use that timeline as the basis for your review, checking on your own progress, identifying challenges and recommitting to your goals as needed.

Keeping those goals front and center will be helpful to staying the course. If you find you're wavering, perhaps the best course of action is to refocus on the exercises you completed in the Audacity section. There I asked you about the impact these changes on the path to Absolute

Engagement would have on you, your business, your team and your clients. The answers to those questions comprise your *why* and will serve as your North Star throughout this process. You may need to reconnect with your *why* on a regular basis.

The Decision

At this point you've worked through the first four steps: awareness, audacity, action and, now, accountability. As you complete step four, you'll come to the next crossroads. Your decision is this:

Will you formalize a process of connecting with peers who will support and push you to succeed? Or will you tough it out and hope that you can do it alone?

In the next chapter we'll look at how to ensure that you have the energy and creativity you'll need to make this happen.

The Recap

- Accountability is about ensuring that you have the personal support you need to follow through on your goals. This is where commitment lives.

- If you do not have a person or group that actively supports you in succeeding you have less chance of success.

- Mastermind groups provide a structure and process that uses a group dynamic to ensure you do not fail.

- Personal accountability will require that you set time aside to focus on your plan and reconnect with the reasons why you are pursuing the path to Absolute Engagement.

- You must decide if you'll continue to work alone, or reach out and create a formal support network that will ensure that you reach your goals.

Your Turn

In this step your goal is to focus on yourself and what you need to accomplish your goals. Specifically, you looked at formalizing a process to create personal accountability. It will be easy to set this chapter aside and tell yourself it's more important to focus on the business. I'd encourage you to make sure you lay a strong foundation for yourself to create the capacity you need to execute on everything you've thought about up to this point.

Download the full workbook at www.absoluteengagement.com/book and enter the code 'IfNotNow'. The workbook includes room to respond and tips to interpret your answers.

Who provides you with the most meaningful support when it comes to achieving your goals?

_____

_____

_____

_____

_____

What is the best way for you to get on-going support (e.g., talk to your spouse, meet with a friend, create or join a Mastermind Group)?

_____

_____

_____

_____

_____

Who would you ideally like to participate in a Mastermind Group that you create?

_____

_____

_____

_____

_____

THE PURSUIT OF ABSOLUTE ENGAGEMENT

How often, when and where will you review your goals as it relates to the pursuit of Absolute Engagement?

_____

_____

_____

_____

_____

Now that you have a good understanding of how to create personal accountability, will you formalize a process of connecting with peers who will support and push you to succeed? Or will you tough it out and hope that you can do it alone?

◯ Yes, I'm continuing down the path to Absolute Engagement

◯ No, my comfort zone is looking good right now

What do you see as the potential barriers at this stage?

_____

_____

_____

_____

_____

What are the specific next steps you will take based on what you have read in this chapter and written about your own business?

1. _____
2. _____
3. _____
4. _____
5. _____

YOUR PATH TO ABSOLUTE ENGAGEMENT

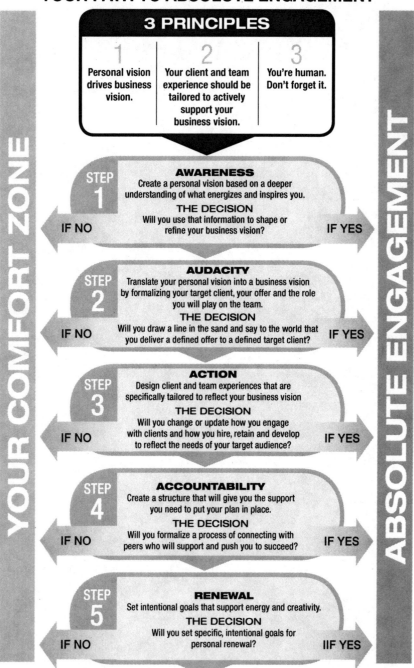

3 PRINCIPLES

1 Personal vision drives business vision.

2 Your client and team experience should be tailored to actively support your business vision.

3 You're human. Don't forget it.

YOUR COMFORT ZONE

ABSOLUTE ENGAGEMENT

STEP 1
AWARENESS
Create a personal vision based on a deeper understanding of what energizes and inspires you.
THE DECISION
Will you use that information to shape or refine your business vision?
IF NO   IF YES

STEP 2
AUDACITY
Translate your personal vision into a business vision by formalizing your target client, your offer and the role you will play on the team.
THE DECISION
Will you draw a line in the sand and say to the world that you deliver a defined offer to a defined target client?
IF NO   IF YES

STEP 3
ACTION
Design client and team experiences that are specifically tailored to reflect your business vision
THE DECISION
Will you change or update how you engage with clients and how you hire, retain and develop to reflect the needs of your target audience?
IF NO   IF YES

STEP 4
ACCOUNTABILITY
Create a structure that will give you the support you need to put your plan in place.
THE DECISION
Will you formalize a process of connecting with peers who will support and push you to succeed?
IF NO   IF YES

STEP 5
RENEWAL
Set intentional goals that support energy and creativity.
THE DECISION
Will you set specific, intentional goals for personal renewal?
IF NO   IIF YES

Complete the steps and you'll be at the intersection of financial success and personal fulfillment. The Absolutely Engaged report higher revenue, less stress, better health and more time spent doing the work they love.

226

11
RENEWAL:
THIS IS WHERE
CREATIVITY LIVES

STARTING POINT:
You've designed a plan to ensure
that your business supports
the life you want to live and the
structure to keep you on track.

THE NEXT STEP:
Set intentional
goals that support
energy and
creativity.

We've made it to Step Five on the path to Absolute Engagement – that's the last one, folks! You're almost there. Renewal is about refueling and reenergizing. And it's critical, because you can put on a red cape but that doesn't make you invincible. Even Superman had to go to his Fortress of Solitude and regroup from time to time. If you're an entrepreneur, or have an entrepreneurial role within a larger organization, you bear a lot of responsibility. You can't engage if you drive yourself into the ground. It's not simply because you get weak and tired (we all do) but because you can lose your creative edge.

Renewal acknowledges that in order to sustain momentum you need to refuel and recharge. It's about recognizing (perhaps reluctantly) that none of us are super heroes, and finding the space to reflect on your vision and fuel your capacity to push forward. This is where creativity lives, because renewal provides you with the mental space you need to focus on the big picture rather than being pulled too far down into the weeds. Those who are Absolutely Engaged are as intentional about the time they take off as the time they are working. In this step you'll set intentional goals to refresh and renew in order to create the capacity in your life to focus on your bigger professional and personal goals.

"I'm So Busy"

Let's face it, we live in a world in which being busy is a badge of honor. When asked how we're doing, we rarely focus on how we're actually feeling, but tend to share the details of our schedule, all the time smiling because we're just a little proud of operating beyond our personal capacity.

Arguments have been made that this culture we've created is unhealthy and authors such as Greg McKeown, who wrote the best-seller *Essentialism*[19], have made compelling arguments that we need to cut back and focus on the right things. I don't doubt for a moment that this approach is important and that we'd all likely be much happier if we followed McKeown's advice.

There are, however two types of busy—one is structural and the other is self-imposed. You probably need to deal with the structural issues, at which point you may be forced to look yourself in the mirror and realize that you're creating the problem.

- Structural busyness is usually a capacity problem. If you're operating over your capacity, this entire process will be in vain because you simply can't deliver. You owe it to yourself to ensure that you have a clear picture of your own capacity. That involves doing the math on how much time you invest in delivering services to your clients relative to the amount of time you can invest in clients, while still leaving yourself the time you need to grow and manage the business.

- Self-imposed busyness comes from a belief that we need to manage and control everything in our lives and that the world may very well stop spinning if we aren't supervising it. If you noted a hint of sarcasm, it was intentional.

Renewal is very much about recharging but that doesn't necessarily mean it's about resting. For many of us, rest is the missing ingredient and sleep is the answer. For others, renewal is more about addressing an imbalance in our lives between work and everything else that's important. In this case renewal may be very active, but it ensures that all of this activity isn't focused on one aspect of our lives, while we ignore the rest.

Get Intentional About Renewal

There's no one way to refresh, recharge or renew. The options are as varied as the readers of this book. One thing, however, is true: We need to be intentional about how we do it. Most of us allow everything else in our lives to take priority over our need to take care of ourselves. We squeeze our own needs around everything else, and our personal time is the first thing to go when we get busy at work. We tell ourselves that we're doing the right thing and take a certain amount of pride in the role we play as martyr to the needs of others. It's time to stop the madness!

Time Off

Something more and more great advisors are doing is setting a big goal for renewal, just as they set audacious goals for their business. Some larger professional firms have even started to mandate sabbaticals for senior staff that may go as long as 30 consecutive days every few years. In our research, only seven percent of advisors indicated that they had taken a sabbatical and the numbers were roughly equivalent across all types of advisors. Clearly, this is an idea more of us need to consider.

There are two reasons why I believe sabbaticals can be a powerful driver of renewal.

1. They provide perspective. After a while, the four walls of our office, our

industry or our lives start to feel all too familiar. The lack of change can literally stop the creative juices from flowing—but flow they will if you can get yourself out of the familiar.

Earlier I talked about Jon Jones, the co-CEO of Brighton Jones, and the success he has had in building his offer (legacy planning) to reflect his passion (charity). In my conversation with Jon he told me that his entire family took a full year and traveled the world. The children were home-schooled for the year and he kept in touch with the business. The vast majority of people would never even consider attempting this but it was a dream the family shared. Had they waited for the time to do this to magically appear, they would still be waiting. Instead, the goal forced Jon to make a lot of changes in his life and business, specifically as it related to structuring a team that could be accountable in his absence. Setting this "big goal" meant building the business and structuring their lives in very specific ways.

2. Sabbaticals force you to organize your business so that it doesn't require your personal touch each and every minute of the day. In order to make a year-long trip possible, Jones would have to be able to delegate and rely on his processes so that he could step away without everything crumbling. He had built the business with a partner, a strategy that supported this kind of adventure. He delegated everything that he could and found a process of staying in touch on the important issues. He communicated with the key stakeholders of the business to reassure them that everything would continue as normal. In short, Jones created a structure that supported his ability to execute on this significant life goal. This is a wonderful example of Absolute Engagement in action.

Too many of us seem to think that vacation time is for the weak. A 2016 study from Allianz Travel Insurance[20] highlighted the fact that over half (53 percent) of Americans had not taken any time off in the last year. Over a third (37 percent) hadn't taken a vacation in more than two years.

According to the study, this downward trend has been noticeable for the last 30 years. The reasons for the decline? We don't believe anyone else can do our work, we want to prove ourselves and we fear the pile of work that might be waiting for us upon our return.

The Absolutely Engaged take a different approach. In our study, those who are Absolutely Engaged are nearly two times as likely to take five or more weeks off each year as the rest of the respondents. What is also striking is that they are more likely to take multiple weeks off at a time. A quarter of the Absolutely Engaged had taken four weeks off at one time compared with 13 percent of all others.

"I take five weeks (or more) off each year."

52%
27%

Absolutely Engaged   All others
Source: AbsoluteEngagement.com

Renewal doesn't require traveling the world. You might be refreshed by something much less dramatic like taking time off work to read, exercise, commit to time with friends or be present with your family. That takes us to the next discussion, about managing energy across different aspects of our lives.

Focus on Energy

As you think about renewal, you may experience this blinding flash of the obvious—we ask too much of ourselves. Jim Loehr is the author of an extraordinary book called *The Power of Full Engagement*[21]. Loehr spent a good part of his career training elite athletes on how to improve their game. What's interesting is that he did not train them on anything related to the technical aspects of their sport; instead, he focused on how they manage their energy.

Loehr makes the great point that elite athletes spend 90 percent of their time training to exert themselves 10 percent of the time. And yet somehow we expect ourselves to be on top of our game for eight, nine or 10 hours a day. With this point he's underlining the critical need for rest after periods of exertion. If you strain a muscle and then give it enough time to recover, you make the muscle stronger and more resistant. According to Loehr this same theory applies to our professional and personal lives. You need to push yourself mentally and physically with the important caveat that you need to balance that with sufficient recovery time.

What's critical to the concept of full engagement—and to this concept of Absolute Engagement—is that it reminds us that renewal is not necessarily a passive activity. There are two elements of Loehr's work that I believe are significant in your pursuit of Absolute Engagement.

1. We can't manage energy if we're focusing all of it in one area of our lives. In fact, Loehr suggests, we need to be physically energized, emotionally connected, mentally focused and spiritually aligned.

2. In order to renew and refresh we don't need to plunk ourselves on the couch with a bag of chips and the remote. In fact, Loehr suggests that to manage our energy we need to create stress—but in a good way. He points out that energy diminishes with both overuse and with underuse of any muscle. He applies that same theory beyond our physical energy and suggests that we need to balance energy expenditure (stress) with renewal.

That holds true, he says, when it comes to almost every aspect of our lives, including our personal relationships. Stated simply, Loehr is asking you to push yourself outside of your comfort zone in all aspects of your life in order to create the energy you need for sustained performance—and in order to refresh and renew. That comes with the caveat that the "push" must be followed by recovery time.

At a minimum, we know that those who are Absolutely Engaged push themselves hard on physical activity.

"I exercise four times or more a week."

61%

42%

Absolutely Engaged   All others

Source: AbsoluteEngagement.com

Get Some Sleep

A Gallup poll[22] suggested that 40 percent of Americans are sleep deprived, which is defined as routinely sleeping less than seven hours a night. I can almost hear you laughing—if that's the standard then call me sleep deprived. And while many of us get less than the recommended number of hours, we're generally okay with that and don't believe that more sleep would have a significant positive impact.

At some point we need to realize that this issue is taking a significant toll on our ability to function, our health and our creativity. The concept of Absolute Engagement recognizes that if you need to suffer to achieve, you're going about it the wrong way.

Ariana Huffington, founder of *The Huffington Post* and author of several well-regarded books, has become the self-declared ambassador of getting more sleep. This became her focus after a personal experience when she, quite literally, fainted from exhaustion. What's most striking about Huffington's approach to sleep is how intentional she is. In her book *The Sleep Revolution: Transforming Your Life One Night at a Time* [23], she describes the ritual, the environment and the comfy jammies, all designed to support a good night's sleep.

So many of us have grown up believing that sleep is wasted time, something reserved for the lazy or unambitious. Huffington points out, however, that "sleep time is not empty time. It involves intense neurological activity that we can think of as cognitive maintenance or personal sustainability." In fact, in her Ted Talk on the subject, *How to Succeed? Get More Sleep,* she refers to sleep as the one best performance enhancer.

While I didn't ask the Absolutely Engaged how much they sleep get, they did report that they were less likely to feel completely exhausted at the end of the day (1 percent compared with 12 percent of all others). They also reported that they were less likely to feel tired when they woke up in the morning (18 percent compared with 38 percent of all others).

There's also research that suggests more sleep will make you a better leader and that has important implications for both your team and your clients. In an article in the *Harvard Business Review*, Nick van Dam and Els van der Helmut (respectively the chief learning officer and sleep specialist with McKinsey Consulting in Amsterdam) bring the connection to life. "Basic visual and motor skills deteriorate when people are deprived of sleep," they say, "but not nearly to the same extent as higher-order mental skills[24]". They point out that the brain functions that take place in the prefrontal cortex (like problem-solving and reasoning) don't do well without sleep. Despite the connection to effective leadership, I'm reticent to go down that utilitarian path because I believe that rest and renewal should be a gift that you give yourself. If we sleep to be better for others, rather than ourselves, we have probably lost the connection to Absolute Engagement.

One of the clear impacts of renewal is that it helps us create meaningful boundaries in our lives. We love to be working and we love to return home. We're energized and present in both situations.

Why Is Renewal So Hard?

At the outset of this journey I made the comment that the two toughest steps on the path to Absolute Engagement were the first and the last. The first step, Awareness, is difficult because we have a difficult time giving ourselves permission to dream and open our minds to the possibility of something more. The last step, Renewal, is difficult because we have to battle demons that tell us to focus on others to the exclusion of ourselves. For some this latter issue is a passing nuisance and can be easily overcome with some stern self-talk. For others, myself included, this runs far deeper.

The reason that renewal is hard is the same reason that Absolute Engagement is hard; it requires us to prioritize our own needs. It's no coincidence that the process is book-ended by steps that demand deep introspection. We all arrive at this place for different reasons:

- We were told that focusing on our needs is selfish.

- We've spent a lifetime building a business and raising a family and have forgotten that we matter as well.

- We don't feel we can stop, even for a minute, because we fear that things will come crashing down.

- We like the fact, if we're honest, that people need us so much we can't take a moment for ourselves—we feel indispensable.

In an interview on her book[25], Daring Greatly, Brené Brown talked openly about her own struggles and said, "I trusted my professional self, but not my personal self." Many of you will understand what this means immediately and a lucky few will think I'm speaking a foreign language. We trust our professional selves and so we pour everything into perfecting that individual. That perfection comes at the cost of our personal selves because we don't trust that that person is as worthy.

And so while I struggle with this step, I'm a researcher at heart and I believe the data. And so I say this with all the humility that comes with past failures; we need renewal to make this work.

The Decision

As you complete Step Five, you'll come to the next crossroads. Your decision is this:

Will you set specific goals for personal renewal? Or, will you continue to try and squeeze this activity around everything else you are doing, leaving it at the bottom of your list?

And that, my friends, is the final decision. We began this process by opening our eyes to the possibility that building a business around a personal vision could lead to profoundly meaningful results for your business and your life. We've walked through five steps to achieve Absolute Engagement, and the five decisions that will keep you moving or send you back to your comfort zone. Now it's all up to you.

The Recap

- Renewal acknowledges that in order to sustain momentum you need to refuel and recharge. This is where creativity lives.

- Those who are Absolutely Engaged set intentional goals around renewal, in particular by taking more vacation.

- Renewal is driven more by managing your energy across four distinct parts of your life: physical, emotional, mental and spiritual. Managing energy demands stressing each area following by periods of rest and recovery.

- Lack of sleep has a negative impact on productivity and creativity.

- Many find renewal one of the hardest steps because it requires that we put ourselves first.

- You must decide if you'll continue to squeeze in time for yourself as you build the business or whether you will intentionally set goals for renewal in the same way you set goals for the business.

Your Turn

In this step we examined the ways in which you can limit energy and creativity and the steps you can take to set intentional goals that support both. Will you give yourself permission to focus on your own needs?

Download the full workbook at www.absoluteengagement.com/book and enter the code 'IfNotNow'. The workbook includes room to respond and tips to interpret your answers.

How much time did you take off last year? _____**weeks**

What was the longest you were off at one time? _____**weeks**

How would you spend your time if you could take more time off?

_____

_____

_____

_____

_____

What would need to happen to allow you to take more time off or more consecutive weeks off?

_____

_____

_____

_____

_____

Do you feel you are balanced in terms of stretching yourself physically, emotionally, mentally and spiritually? Which parts of your life are over-used and which are under-used?

_____

_____

_____

_____

_____

RENEWAL: THIS IS WHERE CREATIVITY LIVES

If you could set a clear goal in each area of your life, outside of work, what would it be?

Physical

_____

_____

_____

_____

_____

Emotional (Relationships)

_____

_____

_____

_____

Mental (Intellectual)

_____

_____

_____

_____

Spiritual

_____

_____

_____

_____

What would the impact be of focusing more time and attention on those other aspects of your life?

_____

_____

_____

_____

THE PURSUIT OF ABSOLUTE ENGAGEMENT

If you could take action on just one goal, which would have the greatest impact?

_____

_____

_____

_____

How much sleep do you get, on average? _____hours

If under 7 hours a night, what could you do to get more sleep?

_____

_____

_____

_____

_____

Now that you have a sense of the things you can do to feed your energy and creativity, will you set specific goals for personal renewal? Or, will you continue to try and squeeze this activity around everything else you are doing, leaving it at the bottom of your list?

○ Yes, I'm continuing down the path to Absolute Engagement

○ No, my comfort zone is looking good right now

What do you see as the potential barriers at this stage?

_____

_____

_____

_____

_____

What are the specific next steps you will take based on what you have read in this chapter and written about your own business?

1. _____
2. _____
3. _____
4. _____
5. _____

PART FIVE:
YOUR COMMITMENTS

The work you have done to this point is real and it's meaningful. Now you'll need to dig deep and make some commitments to yourself to take action.

12
YOUR COMMITMENTS

You have a choice now.

Will you bring your vision to life by pursuing Absolute Engagement or will you head back to your comfort zone? Think back to what it felt like to imagine building a business around your passion and recall the profound impact of Absolute Engagement on the businesses and lives of those who have gone in that direction.

We've examined the path to Absolute Engagement in significant detail. But remember: it all began with three fundamental choices.

- **Will you work with the right clients?** The Absolutely Engaged have identified the clients they are passionate about working with, for whom they can do their best work and who need what they offer.

- **Will you do the right work?** The Absolutely Engaged have made a decision to focus on the kind of work they want to do for clients.

- **Will you play the right role?** The Absolutely Engaged have identified the role they want to play on the team, specifically the work that will help drive the business forward.

Once you've made the decision to build your business around your personal vision, everything else is execution. And once you make the choice to act, you'll not only see a profound impact on your business and your life but you will, perhaps inadvertently, become an inspiration for your team, your clients (and your friends and your kids).

I believe that change is only possible if you:

- stop allowing the past to create your direction in future

- start with a clean slate

- open your mind to possibility

- recognize the need for alignment between what's important in your life and how you run your business

- accept the possibility that if you focus time and attention on the things for which you have the most passion, you'll significantly increase your chances of success

With each step you'll be faced with a critical decision. Hopefully the map on the facing page will help you see the path from here to Absolute Engagement.

The Recap

- You will need to make a decision about whether you move forward toward Absolute Engagement or back to your comfort zone.

- Change is only possible if you refuse to give past failures power, start with a clean slate, open your mind to possibility and recognize that there is a connection between how you run your business and how you run your life.

13
THE FULL RECAP

Chapter 1: Life, Discontent and Possibility

- As we become adults, we tend to limit our dreams to the clearly achievable. In the process we put limits on our imagination before we can give ourselves a chance to dream big.

- We start our careers with a clear goal to grow; managing and sustaining that growth knocks us off course.

- At some point fulfillment flatlines, despite continued growth.

- The flatline is the result of drift from our original goals, lack of a clear vision or a change in what is important to us.

- Some advisors pause, recognize they are off course and break through by changing the question from 'how will I grow' to 'what do I want to create'.

- When you reach the fork in the road, you have a choice to pursue Absolute Engagement or slip back into your comfort zone.

- The pursuit of Absolute Engagement changes the trajectory and focuses you on a future that combines significant growth with profound fulfillment.

Chapter 2: Absolute Engagement: A Vision of What's Possible

- Absolute Engagement is about intentionally designing a business that supports the life you (really) want to live and a life that fuels your capacity to do just that.

- About 15 percent of advisors are Absolutely Engaged. They have both defined and are living their ideal as it relates to the clients with whom they want to work, the work they do and the role they play on the team.

- The impact of intentionally designing a business around your ideal work, clients and role includes:

  ° Greater confidence, clarity and control when it comes to professional goals

  ° Greater time spent on the right activities

  ° Greater financial success

  ° The ability to take more time off

  ° Enhanced well-being, including more energy, lower stress and better health

- The reason for such a significant impact is due, at least in part, to creating a business that has clear purpose and reflects what is most important to you.

Chapter 3: The Path and the Pitfalls

- Advisors who are Absolutely Engaged approach their businesses with three common principles:

  ° Personal vision drives business vision.

  ° Your client and team experience should be tailored to actively support your business vision.

  ° You're human. Don't forget it.

- There are five steps on the path to Absolute Engagement, each of which brings you up against an important decision:

- ° Awareness is about understanding what really energizes and inspires you when it comes to your clients, your work and your role.

- ° Audacity is about translating your personal vision into a business vision.

- ° Action is about tailoring your client and team experience to specifically reflect your offer and the unique needs of your target, while freeing you up to take on the role that will push the business forward.

- ° Accountability is all about ensuring that you have the support you need, personally, to follow through on your goals.

- ° Renewal acknowledges that in order to sustain momentum you need to refuel and recharge.

- Three obstacles can thwart your progress: focusing on what you think you "should" do, putting on the armor and ignoring the role of vulnerability in defining a vision for the future.

- Three characteristics should be nurtured to help you succeed: grit, a growth mindset and big goals.

Chapter 4: Awareness: This is where possibility lives

- Awareness is about getting real on what matters, what you want and how you prioritize those things. This is where possibility lives.

- Awareness is difficult because it opens up the possibility of failure, feels selfish and requires extraordinary vision.

- Those who are Absolutely Engaged have answered three questions related to work, clients and role:

- ° With which clients do I most enjoy working and what is common among those individuals?

- ° When was the last time I was completely energized by the work I was doing and what characterized that work?

- ° What are the things that I, and I alone, should be doing to propel the business forward?

- When you're doing the work that energizes and inspires you, you achieve "flow," which propels you forward.

- To achieve Absolute Engagement you need to be wary of two traps: self-editing your goals before you get a change to start pursuing them and ascribing too much value to what you have today.

- You must decide if you'll use the insights you gain from this step to inform your business going forward, or push those feelings to the side and slip back into your comfort zone.

Chapter 5: Audacity: This is where courage lives

- Audacity is about translating your personal vision into a business vision. It's about using the insights you gleaned in the "awareness phase" to formalize your target client, your offer and the role you will play on the team. This is where courage lives.

- Take action by translating your thinking and brainstorming about clients into a clear definition of your target and ideal client. Then, clearly define your offer and the role you will play in delivering on that offer.

- To drive action, define the impact that the right clients, right work and right role will have on you, your business, your clients and your team.

- In order to assess your plan:

- ° Examine the economic opportunity and impact of making changes to your target, offer and role.

- ° Determine if your plan will resonate with your clients, authentically.

- Focusing on a clear target and offer has three primary benefits:

  ○ It taps into your intrinsic motivation and passion.

  ○ It focuses your efforts rather than diffusing them.

  ○ It differentiates you from other advisors.

- You must decide if you'll draw a line in the sand and tell the world that you work with a defined target client to deliver a defined offer.

Chapter 6: Action: This is where confidence lives

- Action is about tailoring your client and team experience to specifically reflect your offer and the unique needs of your target, while freeing you up to take on the role that will push the business forward. This is where confidence lives.

- When there is alignment between personal, client and team engagement you create a form of momentum that propels the business forward.

- Satisfaction and loyalty are no longer enough. Achieving high ratings on these metrics makes you just as good as everyone else—but not distinctive.

- Engagement is the new standard. Engagement creates a fundamentally different, deeper and more connected relationship with your clients.

- Engagement is being disrupted by two trends:

  ○ A shift from client service to client experience. Client service is table stakes but engagement is driven by the right offer and active leadership.

  ○ Co-creation of value focuses on how you work with your clients and your team, and results in a more involved role for both in the creation and delivery of value.

- You need to communicate your plans to the team prior to defining the client experience but after defining your vision.

- You must decide if you're willing to change how you communicate with clients and how you recruit and develop your team to ensure that the business reflects your vision.

Chapter 7: Action: The Client Experience

- An extraordinary client experience is intentional, consistent and meaningful, and must be designed to support the needs, goals and aspirations of your ideal client.

- When you build your client experience around the unique needs of your target, you are creating a direct connection between personal vision, business vision and client experience. That is the essence of Absolute Engagement.

- You cannot tell clients what an extraordinary client experience looks like but you can invite them into the conversation to help inform that client experience by following these steps:

  ○ Involve the client in defining "great," using surveys, advisory boards or interviews.

  ○ Design an extraordinary and perfectly tailored client journey that reflects the key touchpoints in a client relationship: introduction, initial contact, onboarding, plan development, reviews, education and appreciation.

  ○ Design the structure you need to bring your client journey to life, including skills, partnerships and processes.

  ○ Measure your progress to ensure that you are on track.

- Ensure that your plan reflects the value of clients to support long-term profitability.

- Communicate your plan to clients with confidence and a clear understanding of the potential impact and objections.

Chapter 8: Action: Your Role

- Absolute Engagement is not only about your clients and your team, but about how you will spend your time.

- When you can focus on the right work, the business will experience significant growth.

- To evaluate your time, put your activities into four quadrants based on the extent to which you are passionate about doing the activity and if someone else can do it.

- Once you have evaluated your activities, ask yourself the critical questions to help you confirm the activities you should be doing, give up activities you shouldn't be doing, identify opportunities to train others on key activities and, sometimes, highlight the need for additional support or resources.

Chapter 9: Action: The Team Experience

- An effective team experience needs to align with your personal vision and is co-created with those around you.

- The team and client experience cannot be managed in isolation because creating value is based on the interaction between the employee and the client.

- To map out an engaged team experience follow these three steps:

  ○ Define your culture to connect your personal vision with the vision you have for your team.

  ○ Get clear on fit by defining who is exactly right for your team based on your culture and your client experience.

- ° Co-create an engaging team experience, including development, involvement, communication, reward and fun.

- Those who are Absolutely Engaged:

  - ° Intentionally design and nurture their team culture

  - ° Engage team members with a focus on mastery, autonomy and purpose

  - ° Invite team input when designing the team experience

  - ° Recognize team members based on how well they reflect the values of the firm

  - ° Measure team engagement on an ongoing basis

  - ° Structure the work required to deliver on the client experience and then assign to the team rather than building the process around existing skills

Chapter 10: Accountability: This Is Where Commitment Lives

- Accountability is about ensuring that you have the personal support you need to follow through on your goals. This is where commitment lives.

- If you do not have a person or group that actively supports you in succeeding you have less chance of success.

- Mastermind Groups provide a structure and process that uses a group dynamic to ensure you do not fail.

- Personal accountability will require that you set time aside to focus on your plan and reconnect with the reasons why you are pursuing the path to Absolute Engagement.

- You must decide if you'll continue to work alone, or reach out and create a formal support network that will ensure that you reach your goals.

Chapter 11: Renewal: This Is Where Creativity Lives

- Renewal acknowledges that in order to sustain momentum you need to refuel and recharge. This is where creativity lives.

- Those who are Absolutely Engaged set intentional goals around renewal, in particular by taking more vacation.

- Renewal is driven more by managing your energy across four distinct parts of your life: physical, emotional, mental and spiritual. Managing energy demands pushing yourself in different areas of your life and then allowing time to recover.

- Lack of sleep has a negative impact on productivity and creativity.

- Many find renewal one of the hardest steps because it requires that we put ourselves first.

- You must decide if you'll continue to squeeze in time for yourself as you build the business or whether you will intentionally set goals for renewal in the same way you set goals for the business.

Chapter 12: Your Commitment

- You will need to make a decision about whether you move forward toward Absolute Engagement or back to your comfort zone.

- Change is only possible if you refuse to give past failures power. Start with a clean slate, open your mind to possibility and recognize that there is a connection between how you run your business and how you run your life.

Chapter 14: Action Plan

Download your full workbook and action plan at
www.absoluteengagement.com/book, using the code "IfNotNow."

14
YOUR ACTION PLAN

At this point you've examined what matters most to you, and what you want to create as part of your pursuit of Absolute Engagement. You've thought about how to ensure that you have support and the personal capacity to move forward. What you haven't done yet is taken action.

As you moved through each of the steps, I've asked you a set of questions to get you started. As a next step, however, you'll want to go deeper on some of those questions, identify where you are today and what needs to change in order to structure this awesome client experience.

Need some help? We've created a full workbook with all the questions in this book, plus room for notes and next steps. You can access that workbook at www.absoluteengagement.com/book ; use the code "IfNotNow." The workbook includes all of the exercises that were at the end of each chapter, with additional detail and room to create your action plan.

Don't forget that Absolute Engagement isn't easy. It will take time, and may take some trial and error. I wrote this book because I believe that we need to have different conversations about what is important in our lives. And I believe that the effort you make will not be wasted. Learning what makes you happy, in work and in life – and then taking action to bring those two things together, will allow you to create the business and life you deserve. I wish you every success.

REFERENCES

Chapter 1

[1] Page 10 - **The hierarchy of needs:** first outlined in Maslow, A.H. (1943). "A theory of human motivation". (pp. 370-396), Psychological Review. 50 (4). Later expanded in Maslow, A.H. (1954). Motivation and personality, New York, NY: Harper

[2] Page 16 - **Crystallization of discontent:** Baumeister, Roy F, Heatherton, Todd F., Weinberger, Joel Lee. (1994). "Can personality change?"(pp. 281-297). Washington, DC, US: American Psychological Association, xiv

[3] Page 17 - **Prospection:** Seligman, Martin E.P., Railton, Peter, Baumeister, Roy F., Sripada, Chandra (2013), "Navigating Into the Future or Driven by the Past" (pp. 119-141), Perspective on Psychological Science 8:119

Chapter 3

[4] Page 46 - **Grit:** Duckworth, Angela L., Peterson, Christopher, Matthews, Michael D., Kelly, Dennis R. (2007), "Grit: Perseverance and Passion for Long-Term Goals", (pp. 1087-1101) Journal of Personality and Social Psychology, Vol. 92. No. 6

[5] Page 47 - **Grit:** Interview with Caroline Miller on AbsoluteEngagement.com "The One Best Predictor of Success" (2015)

[6] Page 48 - **Growth Mindset:** Dweck, Carol S., Mindset: The New Psychology of Success (2008), Ballentine Books

[7] Page 49 - **Messy Middle:** Hyatt, Michael on www.michaelhyatt.com "The Myth of Fun, Fast and Easy (And Why It Keeps You From Getting the Results You Want)"

[8] Page 49 - **'Not Yet' Grade:** Dweck, Carol S. on www.ted.com "The power of believing that you can improve"

[9] Page 50 - **Big Goals:** Locke, Edwin A., Latham, Gary P., (2006), "New Directions in Goal-Setting Theory" (pp. 265-268), Association for Psychological Science, Vol. 15, No. 5

Chapter 4

[10] Page 61 - **Good is Enemy of Great:** Collins, Jim (2001), Good to Great: Why Some Companies Make the Leap and Others Don't, HarperCollins Publishers.

[11] Page 68 - **Flow:** Csikszentmihalyi, M. (1990). Flow: The Psychology of Optimal Experience. New York: Harper and Row

[12] Page 70 - **The Endowment Effect:** Kahneman, Daniel, Knetsch, Jack L., Thaler, Richard H. (1991), "Anomalies: The Endowment Effect, Loss Aversion, and Status Quo Bias", (pp. 193-206), The Journal of Economic Perspectives Vol. 5, No. 1

Chapter 5

[13] Page 93 - **Your Why:** Sinek, Simon (2011) Start With Why: How Great Leaders Inspire Everyone to Take Action, Penguin Books

Chapter 6

[14] Page 114 - **Differentiation:** Financial Planning Association (2016) "Defining and Communicating Your Value" whitepaper from Research and Practice Institute.

[15] Page 116 - **Co-Creation of Value:** Prahalad, C.K., Ramaswamy, Venkat (2004) "Co-Creating Unique Value with Customers", (pp. 4-9) Strategy & Leadership Vol. 32 Iss: 3

Chapter 7

[16] Page 130 - **Advisory Boards:** Financial Planning Association, "Trends in Practice Management: Understanding and Driving Client Value" (2016)

Chapter 9

[17] Page 181 - **Client and Team Connection:** Fleming, John H., Asplund, Jim, (2007), Human Sigma: Managing the Employee-Customer Encounter, Gallup Press

Chapter 10

[18] Page 214 - **Michelangelo Effect:** Drigotas, Stephen, Rusbult, Caryl, Wieselquist, Jennifer, Whitton, Sarah (1999). "Close Partner as Sculptor of the Ideal Self: Behavioral Affirmation and the Michelangelo Phenomenon" (pp 293-323) Journal of Personality and Social Psychology. 77

Chapter 11

[19] Page 226 - **Essentialism:** McKeown, Greg (2014), Essentialism: The Disciplined Pursuit of Less, Crown Publishing Group

[20] Page 228 - **Vacation:** Allianz Travel Insurance (2016) "Vacation Confidence Index"

[21] Page 230 - **Energy:** Loehr, Jim, Schwartz, Tony (2005) The Power of Full Engagement: Managing Energy, Not Time, Is the Key to High Performance and Personal Renewal, The Free Press

[22] Page 231 - **Sleep Deprivation:** Gallup Poll (2013) on www.gallup.com

[23] Page 232 - **Role of Sleep:** Huffington, Arianna (2016) The Sleep Revolution: Transforming Your Life, One Night at a Time, Harmony Books

[24] Page 233 - **Sleep and the Brain:** van Dam, Nick, van der Helmut, Els (2016) "There's a Proven Link Between Leadership and Getting Enough Sleep", Harvard Business Review, February 2016

[25] Page 234 - **Self-Care:** Brown, Brené, Interview with Jonathan Fields for Good Life Project, OWN Network.